Working with Secondary Students who have Language Difficulties

Mandy Brent

Florence Gough

Susan Robinson

David Fulton Publishers

First published 2001
by The Australian Council for Educational Research Ltd
19 Prospect Hill Road, Camberwell, Victoria, 3124

Published in Great Britain (with amendments) by
David Fulton Publishers, 414 Chiswick High Road, London W4 5TF

10 9 8 7 6 5 4 3 2 1

British Library Cataloguing-in-Publication Data
A catalogue record for this book is available from the British Library

ISBN 1 84312 191 3

Printed in Great Britain

Contents

Acknowledgments

The authors gratefully acknowledge the help of Sarah Fulton; Sylvia Walton (Principal of Tintern AGGS); Lyn Henshall (Vice-Principal, Tintern AGGS); Sue Healey (Director of Information Services) and the staff of the Cullen Resource Centre; the many Tintern staff members whose contributions are acknowledged in the text; the students, parents, teachers, and other professional colleagues who have taught us so much; the students who allowed us to include their work (Alexandria Copling, Ellen Davis, Michelle Ross); and our supportive families.

Foreword

The task of teaching children and adolescents with language learning disabilities is complex and at times taxing. It is also a task that must be shared between family and school.

Working with Secondary Students who have Language Difficulties specifically looks at the school area and the management of young people with this disability. It has been a great privilege for me to work within a school setting that has allowed and indeed fostered very strong programmes that are well integrated throughout the curriculum and are designed to assist young people with this particular disability.

Students with language learning disabilities are in every school. It is imperative that there be systems and structures in place to identify their difficulties and assist them in moving through the school system in ways that enhance their capacity to learn. This has led to the need for a whole-school approach, in which the teaching staff are knowledgeable about the students' difficulties and have the capacity to work with specialist staff, particularly in modifying curriculum and assisting young people to understand how they need to learn and compensate.

It has been found that integrating specialist teachers with the staff, and supporting staff and students, both as individuals and in small groups, while keeping the students firmly linked to their class groups and to their timetabled subjects, has the practical benefit of skilling the teaching staff and assisting the students to move to the final years of schooling in a confident manner. By offering this range of different approaches, from individual to group to classroom, young people have quickly learned their own strategies and forms of management. Staff have also been greatly assisted, not only in knowledge and skill, but in supporting these students.

The work that has been done demonstrates that schools benefit from the addition to their team of professionals from other disciplines including speech and language pathology. The benefits gained by staff and students are enormous. The school has the added pleasure of seeing individual students with this very specific disability achieve their goals. Sometimes this involves vocational training courses within the school sector and at other times it leads to final exams.

Finally, it has been my observation that having these students so well organised and integrated into the school community and having a variety of professionals working with teachers has had an extremely positive and practical influence on the teaching staff and students. It has led to important curriculum developments that have benefited every student, not just those for whom the original work was specifically designed. The whole-school approach, with professionals assisting and working with teachers and young people, as well as a school climate that truly values the individual, can promote effective learning not only for adolescents with language learning disabilities, but for all students.

It is a pleasure for me to commend this book by Mandy Brent, Florence Gough, and Sue Robinson and also to compliment the staff of the school for the enthusiastic way in which this programme has been embraced.

Sylvia J. Walton
Principal, Tintern AGGS

Introduction

Language learning disabled students: who are they?

Language is critical for satisfactory progress at school. To cope with the school curriculum, students must be proficient in language in all its forms – speaking, listening, understanding, reading, and writing. It is generally assumed that children arrive at school with normal language. However, some children – more than we often assume – have problems with their language skills. They have difficulties with their mother tongue despite fine minds and good ears.

If apparently alert, capable students have difficulty with understanding or using spoken language – and consequently have difficulty with reading, understanding, and producing written language – it is essential to consider that they might have a language learning disability (LLD).

How do you notice them in school?

Teachers might notice such students because of their poor learning or because of their poor behaviour, but a great concern is that they often 'hide out' in classrooms and go unnoticed. Even if they are noticed, their problems are often misunderstood and the fact that they have language learning disabilities is often not recognised.

Students with language learning disabilities are generally not successful students and often quietly drop out without finishing school. They are over-represented in the number of students who fail to finish school. Students who do not finish school are known to have more difficulties in finding work than students who do finish school.

Some students are experts at covering up; they camouflage their difficulties and draw little attention to themselves. Others do not proceed as quietly. Some of them cause a great deal of disruption at school, particularly after the mid primary years. The skills they need for success at school are not developing, they are often confused and in trouble for not doing what they should, and they often have considerable difficulty with social skills and peer relationships. Their self-esteem is poor, and is precarious as they enter adolescence – a phase of their lives when personal identity and establishing a sense of self is a major goal.

Schools easily recognise negative behaviour, but the fact that this behaviour is caused by serious underlying difficulties with language often goes unnoticed. These language difficulties make the regular curriculum inaccessible and the school environment extremely frustrating.

How is language linked to learning?

Language is critical for learning and underpins everything that goes on at school. From the beginning, children use language to communicate – to tell stories, to pass on information and to question. Teachers use language to chat, to explain, to instruct, to direct, to discipline and to reason. Language is necessary for social interaction and for formal learning. At first, children use their language to talk about the 'here and now' – asking for things, greeting, and making comments. Then they move on to develop more sophisticated language that becomes the basis for the complex skills required for learning. Language underpins memory and makes it possible to develop higher-level mental operations or thinking skills – such as planning, reasoning and reflecting on issues and events. It is essential to recognise that spoken language is the foundation for written language.

Language travels along a continuum – from oral language used to communicate to written language used to educate and become educated. Difficulties with reading, writing and spelling are often part of a bigger picture of language disability that must be considered in planning for the education of these students.

What problems do they have?

Vocabulary

LLD students often have a limited vocabulary and are slow to recognise the meaning of words. They tend to be concrete in their interpretation of the meaning of words and tend to attach only one meaning to a specific word. If the meaning they put on a word does not make sense, they cannot think of another possible meaning or infer what it might mean. They then become confused and frequently 'tune out'. This happens with both spoken and written language.

Language of learning

In addition to everyday language, students need the specific vocabulary and language of different subject areas. There is also a whole special 'language of learning' that students need to understand to be able to take tests, write assignments and understand textbooks. Students might know quite a lot but have difficulty revealing what they know because they cannot understand the language of the test or the assignment. They might know a lot about the topic but might not know what to do unless the question is rephrased.

'Reading between the lines'

Understanding language is very complex. It is necessary not only to understand the overt meaning of words heard or read, but also to appreciate that important details are often implied, and not expressed in words. For understanding, students must 'read between the lines'.

Understanding spoken language

Students with an LLD have trouble picking up the information that is all around them in conversations, discussions, news snippets and talks. They pick up only bits and pieces; they miss a lot. The bits and pieces that they do pick up might not be the most important – indeed they might be minor or 'throw-away' snippets of information. Students make an effort to put these pieces together, but their conclusions can be way 'off beam'. In most cases, they think it is normal to be surrounded by language that they do not understand and they are often unaware that they have not understood.

Speed of processing language

To be understood, language must be processed quickly, constantly, and 'on-line'. Language is not like a machine operated by a coin in a slot – in which everything falls into place at the moment when the handle is turned and the coin drops down. Students who do not process and understand language *continuously*, drop out of the comprehension process very early. They have difficulty understanding and picking out salient points. They might get the gist of things going on around them, but they have trouble getting a grip on the details.

Teenage language

As students grow older, their language becomes more complex and sophisticated. Students have to deal with figurative language, humour and slang. To function appropriately in social situations they also have to know how to talk to whom. This can be difficult for LLD students, who can thus be considered insolent or indifferent.

It is common for teachers to say that a particular student does not have trouble with his or her spoken language: 'He can talk about football just fine'. In making this observation, teachers are saying that such students can engage in simple conversational language if they know something about the topic. But so can a seven-year-old child. The language needed for learning is much more sophisticated than this.

LLD students do not master the more sophisticated forms of social and written language that they need if they are to deal with the curriculum as they progress through school.

When does a language learning disability begin?

Signs of a language disability can be seen in the early years of development. Children might be slow to talk and slow to combine words into grammatical sentences. They might have difficulty understanding things that are said to them and they might learn to camouflage this fact by watching others.

Children who have a history of delay or difficulty with spoken language development (which might or might not affect the clarity of their speech) are in a high-risk group for literacy difficulties and learning difficulties – even if their language has improved by the time that they start school. Another indicator of high risk is the presence of family members with language or learning difficulties. For some children, the difficulties become apparent only as they grow older, or when they begin to learn to read and write.

What happens over time?

Do children mature and grow out of these problems? On the whole, they do not. It is natural to hope that, as spoken language starts to improve, other aspects of language will also develop normally. But a disability that begins by affecting spoken language usually goes on to become a lifelong problem. Because it affects school learning, it is called a 'language learning disability'. Language is an underlying factor in many learning difficulties and, today, literacy problems are considered to be an aspect of a wider language disorder.

About this book

The book is divided into three parts.

Part I The Language Learning Disabled Student

Part I presents readers with a short summary of current information about LLD students in a quickly accessible and readable form – including the learning characteristics of these students, the recognition of these students in the classroom, and an account of their social, emotional, and developmental needs. Examples from students illustrate this information.

Part II Teaching the Language Learning Disabled Student

Part II considers key issues that arise for students and outlines practical suggestions for use in the classroom. How can a teacher create the best learning environment? What should the teacher focus on? There are effective strategies to help students become more organised and independent, to assist comprehension, and to improve written work.

Part III Modifying the Curriculum

The third part deals with taking the existing curriculum and changing it in ways that will allow success for LLD students. This is an area in which teachers frequently ask for help and the authors have therefore been ambitious and included many suggestions derived from practical experience. We have used the term 'modification' – although this sits somewhat uneasily. A better description is 'curriculum development'. A differentiated curriculum to allow for individual differences is well accepted and developing curriculum for students with LLD should fall within this concept. However, 'modification' is the term that has come to be accepted and its use is continued in this book.

This third part of this book would not exist without the teamwork of the many teachers who have recognised the difficulties of their students and who, from their subject knowledge and teaching expertise, have come up with many good ideas. To support LLD students successfully, an integrated approach is necessary. This includes direct work with students, the development of appropriate curriculum in all subject areas, and a supportive school policy endorsed by senior administration.

PART 1

The Language Learning Disabled Student

*y LLD students have difficulty generating vocabulary and
can cause difficulties in getting started on the research process.
event their feeling overwhelmed by the task, it is important to
up skills slowly. There are additional steps that can be added
e students confront text.*

PLANNING
REASONING
REFLECTING

limited vocabulary   meaning of words

CHAPTER 1

Language Development and LLD – What Goes Wrong?

Limits of language development

In the past, it was often said that language had developed to its limit by the early primary school years. This is not the case: language continues to develop through to mature years. But it is not as easy to recognise the growth of language in adolescence as it is to recognise the rapid growth of language that is obvious in a child's early years.

For young children, mastering spoken language is the most important language goal. For school-age students the most important language goal is to develop more sophisticated oral language and to convert this into written forms.

What happens to language in adolescence?

Written language becomes very important in adolescence. Indeed, it is much more important in adolescence than in childhood. Adolescents are expected to read complex material and to write in a sophisticated manner about various, often abstract, topics. Skilful use of written language becomes more important for accessing information through the use of sources such as computers and the Internet. Accessing information independently is vital for learning.

Adolescents need to be able to follow many formal and informal styles of language – from the formal instructional language that they encounter in textbooks to the 'teenlang' of their friendship groups. Language is needed to plan and organise, to solve problems and to reason. Adolescents must not only *use* written and spoken language, but they must also *think* about the language that is used. They need to analyse the style, effect and appropriateness of language in school activities such as film or novel study.

As they grow older, adolescents need to recognise and understand the hidden messages that are not put directly into words. They have to learn to 'read between the lines' and consider the possibility of alternative meanings in what they read and hear. A solid basis of language is required to develop such abstract thinking skills.

Adolescents need to deal with different teachers and different content areas. Teachers in secondary school approach teaching using different language styles and focus more on content. To cope with this, students need to produce more language and to become better organised and fluent with language in its many different forms.

The face of language disabilities in adolescence

If children who have language disabilities have suitable help from an early age, they will progress over the years and master many language skills. But it is rare for such students to 'catch up' with peers completely. Ahead of the students, and always out of reach, language continues to develop and to become more sophisticated. To learn more advanced language one needs a good foundation of language. It is an elusive goal. By adolescence, a child who started out with a language disorder tends to become a teenager with a language-based learning disability (or language learning disability; LLD).

Language problems become learning problems

Students who struggle with LLD commonly have difficulties in their school lives. They often find schoolwork frustrating. Their constant exposure to failure undermines their self-esteem, and they are likely to feel bad about themselves and to drop out before they finish school. It is tempting to think that school is not the place for them and that perhaps they would be better off leaving school and finding a job. But students who do not complete their schooling are likely to find difficulty in getting a job. The passage towards emotional and financial independence is often rocky. Unemployment, disillusionment, and poverty can be just around the corner.

There are many causes of functional illiteracy, but LLD is one of the most important. Adolescents grow and develop language skills, but language disabilities do not disappear.

Language learning disabled students

Language learning disabilities occur when individuals with apparently average general ability have unexpected difficulty learning from existing curriculum and teaching practice at school. Approximately 10–16 per cent of students have a specific learning problem. Not all struggling students have specific learning disabilities. Problems can also be caused by social and emotional difficulties, frequent absences, poor teaching, and a mobile life style.

The following features are commonly noted in students with LLDs:

- academic delay – particularly poor comprehension, reading, and writing affecting subjects across the curriculum;
- competence in some practical aspects of development (for example, sport or graphics), but less competence in other areas;
- learning difficulties that are not caused by emotional disturbance, intellectual handicap, hearing loss, or English as a second language (although some of these factors might exist in some students with LLD: that is, students who have one or more of these other difficulties can also have LLD);

- learning difficulties that cannot be traced to environmental disadvantage.
- males are more likely to present with problems than females;
- although they have some features in common, students with LLD show diverse characteristics.

Language disability is the most common problem reported among students described as 'learning disabled'.

Students with LLD might have brains that process information in a different way. This difference causes difficulties in processing language signals rapidly and proficiently. With access to new technology it is possible to watch what is happening in the brain while it is working. Learning language requires the brain to process the many rapidly changing sounds that make up individual words and the strings of words that form sentences. Difficulties in processing these sounds undermine the development of spoken and written language.

Many LLD students also experience delays in acquiring speech and language. Children who have oral language problems are likely to experience reading, writing and spelling problems even if they are speaking well when they start school. By early evaluation of language skills, it is now possible to identify these children before they start school.

These students might also have an inherited genetic link, although the pattern of difficulties shown by individual family members varies.

LLD continues throughout a person's life, but changes over time. Although the precise difficulties with language vary, the common result is students with poor social skills, low self-esteem, and other emotional and behavioural problems.

Some students have no noticeable early problems with spoken language. Problems can show up later when students try to learn to read, or have to translate their oral ideas into written language.

Although the problems experienced by students with LLD might seem daunting, they are able to learn. This book shows how you can help these students to make the most of their learning opportunities in secondary school.

LLD students have difficulty generating vocabulary and
cause difficulties in getting started on the research process.
nt their feeling overwhelmed by the task, it is important to
skills slowly. There are additional steps that can be added
udents confront text.
PLANNING
REASONING
REFLECTING

Characteristics of Students with LLD

Individuals and the group

When dealing with students with LLD, it is important to remember that each student is an individual with individual problems and that each student's language and learning profile is therefore different. It is not possible to make sweeping generalisations about the members of a group characterised by such diversity. Although many of the following features might appear to be a normal part of growing up, the magnitude and persistence of these characteristics in LLD students seriously interferes with learning.

Disorganised in time

Students with LLD are often disorganised in time and they can have difficulty understanding timetables.

Students with LLD:

- frequently turn up late to class and appointments;
- do not know where they should be at given times;
- can totally forget arrangements unless reminded immediately beforehand; and
- need reminding to consult timetables to find out information about rooms and times.

Kerry is fifteen years old, and is in third year. She is a sociable and motivated student with a keen interest in sport and graphics.

Kerry has the ability to converse about day-to-day things but, because her oral language skills are not sophisticated, she has difficulty with tasks such as explaining, describing, presenting an oral argument, and justifying an opinion.

Kerry is also a poor speller and has difficulty producing written language. She can write a letter in a satisfactory fashion but she has trouble in more sophisticated skills including the development of a storyline, the analysis of characters and the presentation of a discussion.

She is a slow reader and makes many mistakes when she reads (although the extent of these problems depends on what she is reading). She does not enjoy reading. When she has finished reading a section of text, she feels that she has not grasped the meaning.

As well as being disorganised in such matters as timetables, students with LLD are often inefficient with their use of time in other respects.

Students with LLD:

- waste time in class;

- are slow to get started on tasks;

- do not achieve enough in the given time; and

- become excellent procrastinators.

With regard to the last point, LLD students often spend long periods of time looking for things in a pencil-case, or writing and erasing constantly. Such procrastination is an avoidance strategy to deal with difficult tasks – by looking busy but achieving little.

Peter comes to class and puts his head down, apparently working. But if we watch him closely we see that he spends half the lesson doing things such as:
- 'organising' his papers;
- finding things in his folder;
- writing every letter in a different colour;
- erasing endlessly (because his work isn't precisely to his satisfaction).

Students with LLD can also be confused by time indicators. Unless specifically told, they might not appreciate the significance of bells to indicate the start of classes.

Twelve-year-old Andy took no notice when the bell started to ring, calling the students to assemble.

His teacher advised Andy that the bell was telling him to go to class.

'Really?' replied Andy. 'I never realised that was what it meant!'

They can also be unrealistic about the amount of time it takes to complete tasks. Students with LLD:

- do not appreciate how many steps there are in a task and how long each one will take;

- might expect to complete a lengthy assignment in one night;

- do not realise that a two-week timeline means that they should start working immediately, and not leave the work until the last couple of days;

- do not leave enough time to check work; and
- do not allow time for the unexpected, and always presume that things will go smoothly.

> Mary was irritated at being asked to read a chapter of her novel with a teacher.
> 'I can do this. I don't need any help.'
> 'How long do you think it will take you to read this chapter?'
> 'About ten minutes.'
> 'Well read it now and we'll see how long it takes.'
> Mary took forty minutes to read the chapter. It took another ten minutes to make sure that she understood the material.

> Anna, a fifth year, was preparing for a major assessment task. After discussion in class she did not seem to be in a great hurry to get started, although the deadline was four days later.
> 'How long do you think it will take you to do it?'
> 'I'll do it after dinner tonight.'
> 'How long do you think that other students take to finish their assignment?'
> 'I don't know.'
> Despite the fact that this was a task that would realistically take weeks, and despite the fact that the task had been a major topic of study and conversation for a long time, Anna had no realistic understanding of the complex nature of the assignment and the time she would need to complete it.

Disorganised with possessions

Students with LLD often have difficulty keeping track of possessions and require a great deal of monitoring. This can manifest itself in several ways.

Students with LLD:

- often have untidy lockers;
- do not bring appropriate equipment and books to class and do not take such things home to do homework;
- are unaware of the books and materials that they do have;
- lose things frequently (including library books, record books, jumpers, trumpets, and so on);
- have difficulty using folders;
- often do not realise that things have been mislaid; and
- do not take appropriate steps to locate lost property; that is, they have to be supervised to go through appropriate routines (retracing their steps, looking in classrooms, searching lost property, and so on).

Mark brings his English folder to maths, or his computer folder to French, or his history folder to Science. He puts his notes for the class he is attending in whatever folder he happens to have with him.

Sometimes he tucks loose pages in and sometimes he clips them in. If he is worried about losing loose sheets he puts them into his record book. He uses plastic pockets sometimes, but often clips the pockets into his folders upside down.

When Mark picks up his books and folders, it is common for many things to fall onto the floor. Then he gathers them all up quickly and rushes out.

Daniel is twelve years old and is in first year. He is a friendly student and greets his teachers very brightly every time he sees them but he drifts among different friendship peer groups.

Daniel has difficulty in sitting for more than about fifteen minutes in class, and has a short concentration span. He can be disruptive – especially in classes such as drama, dance, music, and ceramics.

Daniel finds reading difficult. He is a slow and hesitant reader and makes many mistakes in oral reading. He reads things but, when he finishes, he doesn't have a clue what he has read about. Daniel doesn't like reading.

His written work is simple. His spelling is weak, and his sentence structure is very basic. He finds difficulty in directly writing answers to questions: he first needs to explain what he wants to write.

Daniel reads instructions, but he does not know what to do when he has finished reading the instructions. After the teacher explains what is required, Daniel looks confused and immediately asks what to do. He is always asking whether what he is doing is right.

He is very slow to master maths processes, frequently asks whether he is doing things properly and forgets many of the content details in class.

At present, Daniel feels that he does not want to be at school after Year 9.

Difficulties structuring work

Students with LLD often have difficulties structuring their work. This aspect of LLD is a reflection of the students' inability to organise ideas and thoughts. It can be exacerbated by poor reading comprehension and poor writing skills.

Students with LLD can:

- have difficulty understanding what they have to do unless it is carefully explained (even if written instructions have been supplied);
- find difficulty in taking steps to assemble information from suitable sources to complete a task;
- have problems with seeing tasks through to completion unless given help to structure the task step by step;
- have difficulty breaking a task into steps and do not ask themselves what they have to do at each step in the process;

- have difficulty in appreciating the overall *need* to plan tasks, actually *organising* such a plan, and understanding the *time involved* to finish each step;
- not always persist with a task to completion, but might hop from one task to another;
- drop a task completely when they strike an obstacle to completing it (they may fail to get assistance when this happens, and apparently need to be taught exactly when and how to ask for help); and
- often lose track of where they are in a task, complete part of it, and fail to return to it – often requiring encouragement to persist ('Don't stop until you have finished what you are doing'), or requiring advice to put a 'post-it' marker in the place to remind them to return to the task later.

> Tom has work to do on a computer at school. Within a short time he is stuck, so he gets up from the computer he is working on and moves to the next one. The same thing happens, so he moves on again.
>
> Within fifteen minutes, Tom has exhausted all available computers. He then occupies himself with other activities.
>
> He takes no action to seek help at any stage.

Disorganised in place

Students with LLD can be very confused in secondary school.

Students with LLD:

- have difficulty in locating classrooms and knowing what to do when there are classroom changes;
- can become proficient over time, but encounter difficulty when they need to adapt to the unexpected (for example, missing the bus and arriving late; or a relocation of a class to a different part of the school; or a change in the daily timetable with the school).

> Anthoula is thirteen years old, and is in second year. She is cheerful and enthusiastic about everything and reports that she is good at everything.
>
> Anthoula works quickly but makes many mistakes. She ticks wrong answers as being correct. She is a weak speller.
>
> Anthoula doesn't ask for help. In fact, she becomes cross when help is offered.
>
> She can make only simple conversation and is often stuck for words – especially when asked to describe things or explain matters.
>
> Anthoula says that she loves reading, but when she recounts a story that she has read, it is a very different account from that of the author.
>
> She laughs heartily when her classmates do, but they do not always seem to enjoy her company and they often avoid her in group work.
>
> She talks a lot in class and does not remember to bring the items she needs. She loses things constantly.
>
> Athoula needs to be reminded about the work she is doing and has a sketchy record book.
>
> She gets into squabbles in sport and feels that other girls cheat or are unfair to her.

Difficulties with comprehension

Students with LLD do not always follow instructions easily.

Typically, students with LLD:

- appear not to listen or appear to be day-dreaming;
- have difficulty in remembering spoken information;
- in conversation, often grasp only the beginning or the end of a sentence;
- grasp only some of the details they hear and cannot accurately combine these fragments of information;
- try to concentrate on what is being said but, because they do not understand all the vocabulary, 'tune out';
- can still be concentrating on the beginning and miss the end;
- do not have a good overall scheme of the topic in mind (such that details that they hear fall into separate fragments and do not integrate into a scheme that they can understand and remember);
- jump to conclusions because of inadequate understanding and inaccurate predictions based on incomplete past knowledge;
- do not understand the meaning of all the words, terms, and concepts used;
- attempt to make sense of what has been said, but put it together incorrectly; and
- do not realise that they have not understood and therefore cannot ask questions to clarify matters.

Being confused is 'normal' for these students. This means that they are often not aware of the nature of their own difficulties and do not develop strategies for identifying when they have insufficient information.

> Lucy says that she 'tries to listen', but she apparently doesn't hear what teachers say.
> 'I thought I was listening, but after class I didn't know what to do. So I guess I can't have been listening.'
> No matter how much she tries, it is only minutes before Lucy feels confused by what the teacher says and is awash with information that she cannot sort out.

> Michael is fourteen and in second year. He is hard-working, courteous and never causes disciplinary problems. He has a big smile but rarely speaks. Michael suffers from headaches at the thought of school.
> Before answering questions, Michael pauses for a long time – so long that the questioner might think that Michael hasn't heard the question or doesn't know the answer. He has difficulty finding the right word and sometimes finding any words at all.
> Michael speaks only in simple sentences and these contain many grammatical errors. His reading is very slow and he cannot read anything independently.
> Michael has difficulty completing much classwork but is very good with his hands and can make things if he understands what to do.

He often misunderstands what people say to him and repeatedly looks around for clues. Michael is slow to start working and waits until others start before he does. He quite likes sport but team sports are a little overwhelming.

Difficulties with vocabulary

Students with LLD can have a restricted vocabulary.

Students with LLD often:

- need assistance to learn the special vocabulary of various subjects and activities (such as science, computing, health, history, and geography);
- confuse words that have more than one meaning;
- do not deduce the meaning of unfamiliar words from the context; and
- confuse words that sound alike (for example, 'conscious'/'conscience'; 'consistent'/'constant'; 'defence'/'defect'; 'silver bean'/'silver beet'.

James and his speech pathologist were talking about words that have double meanings. When asked to put the word 'complimentary' into a sentence to show that he understood the meaning, he responded with:
   'You know it's like in *Sherlock Holmes*, "complimentary my dear Watson".'

Difficulties generalising from specifics

Because they have difficulties generalising from specifics, students with LLD have problems in applying knowledge of skills that they have learned.

Students with LLD:

- cannot automatically carry learned skills into a new situation;
- have difficulty making connections between separate sources of information (for example, a formula sheet might be provided to assist with working out a maths problem, but students might not know how to use this help);
- have difficulty using aids (such as checksheets or formulae sheets) provided by teachers unless someone is there to show the students how to apply the information to the problem in a step-by-step process;
- do not seem to understand cause and effect; and
- do not appreciate the full significance of their actions or the full significance of what they have said.

The librarian showed Sam how to access databases. However, when he has an assignment that requires a search for information, he does not know how to go about it.

Sam has been taught about the contents page of a book, but needs to be directed specifically to look at the contents page to find the information that he needs.

Sam learned about computers in information technology classes, but needs to be prompted constantly to use a computer to produce the text for an assignment.

Sam has been taught to take notes, but he does not think to use notetaking strategies for his assignment.

A long time to process information

To LLD students, a person speaking at a normal rate can seem to be speaking too fast.

Students with LLD:

- need time to think about what has been said;

- need time to digest small portions of information;

- can still be working out one part of the information long after it has passed and can miss information that is presented later;

- need to go over key information (sometimes requiring the information to be simplified if they still don't understand); and

- often need spoken information to be supported with brief notes, diagrams, and keywords.

Shane was asked a question. He thought about it for a long time.

His teacher thought that Shane didn't understand. The teacher therefore rephrased the original question. Shane then had to restart the comprehension process.

It was as though Shane had been asked an entirely new question.

Frequently distracted

LLD students often find difficulty in concentrating. This can be because they:

- have difficulty focusing attention in the face of competing stimulation in the classroom;

- cannot understand and therefore give up;

- cannot complete set tasks and therefore lose interest; and

- have difficulty learning to sustain concentration on tasks.

Students with LLD often need help with tasks and frequently have to wait for this help. For example, if they have major reading difficulties they need someone to read information to them before they can proceed. If they have to wait for this information, they 'learn' to flit from one thing to another.

George is fifteen and in third year. George irritates people because he seems to be rude. When asked about this he becomes very upset and apologises. George is a fringe person; he is tolerated, but is not really favoured in group work.

He is quite bright and is certainly at least 'average'. He is quite good at maths and reads well. George interrupts people repeatedly and talks over them. He doesn't 'tune in' to what other people are speaking about. He contradicts others or laughs at what they say. George is very strong about his own point of view.

He completes much of his work well, but other work is performed haphazardly.

George understands some things but not others. He has particular difficulties with understanding spoken and written language. He can write factual pieces, but finds creative writing difficult.

George doesn't 'catch' jokes. It takes him a while to appreciate the humour of a story. It takes time for 'the penny to drop'; sometimes it never does.

George does not like sport and he wanders at recess and at lunchtime.

Strategies for teaching the LLD student

This book will consider teaching strategies for LLD students in detail in Part 2 (page 23). However, having described the major characteristics of LLD students, it is appropriate at this stage to provide some introductory thoughts on teaching strategies.

The following checklist is designed to provide teachers with some general points to keep in mind when teaching LLD students. Some of these points require very little extra effort on the teacher's part but can make an enormous difference to LLD students. Teachers might feel that they are already doing many of these things in their classes. Indeed they might be, but it should be kept in mind that LLD students require extra explanation and reinforcement. This extra effort can be extremely beneficial.

Organisation

- Teach students how to file and organise handouts and work.
- Acquaint students in a direct way with classroom rules.
- Actively teach study skills. For example, teach note-taking, time management, organisational systems, summary lists and keywords.

Giving instructions to support comprehension

- Explain the purpose of an activity.
- Emphasise information that is important to learn. LLD students are not very good at filtering and cognitively organising information. Repeat advice if necessary.
- Restate, emphasising key points.
- Deliberately slow down the rate of presentation.

- Use shorter units of explanation.
- Limit the amount of new material presented at one time.
- Allow a longer pause time at the end of questions before expecting LLD students to answer.
- Provide a list of vocabulary for a new topic and check students' understanding of these words. Limit the amount of new vocabulary.
- Provide background information and discussion before expecting students to answer. This, together with the provision of the vocabulary needed, gives LLD students the advantage of familiarity with the topic before answering questions.
- Provide visual cues and concrete materials to assist learning and remembering.
- Use gesture and action to enhance the meaning of verbal material.
- Give direct instructions rather than indirect instructions. For example, say 'Quiet please', rather than 'I didn't hear Judy because some people were talking'.
- Avoid sarcasm and ambiguity. Explain and restate metaphorical language. Abstract ideas and language will be problematic, so restate and simplify.

Presenting assignments

- Provide clear written directions and expectations for assignments and projects.
- Support spoken information with written information. Remember that LLD students are slow and inaccurate at transcribing notes from the board.

Completing set work

- Directly teach the skills underlying reading comprehension, maths problem-solving, and so on. This might require the breaking-down of tasks into small steps and the formulation of a plan of action.
- Talk students through a task, describing it step by step while students are performing the task or while the task is demonstrated.
- Provide peer modelling. For example, good examples of answers to questions can be highlighted by teachers and shared with students. Students can then choose those statements that best reflect their own ideas and then edit their original work.
- Negotiate an appropriate amount of work for students to complete.
- Be aware that LLD students might have difficulty with writing. Negotiate other ways of collecting and presenting information.
- Provide a range of materials and activities – from very simple to more difficult so that information is accessible to students.
- Have reasonable time expectations for the completion of the work.
- Emphasise metalinguistic skills to foster independence and analysis. The term 'metalinguistic' refers to the process of reflecting upon language. For example, asking the question: 'What does the word "describe" mean that I have to do?'.

- Encourage and teach a variety of memory strategies: mnemonics, charts, visuals and so on.

Preserving self-esteem

- Provide private negotiation time for LLD students. This addresses not only the students' LLDs, but also the vulnerability of adolescence, which can make direct questioning in front of peers embarrassing.
- Encourage and reward students when they seek help and clarification.

As noted above, these sorts of teaching strategies are discussed in more detail in Part 2 (page 23).

Brooke is sixteen years old. She works hard but lacks confidence.

Brooke finds all schoolwork difficult, with the exception of home economics.

She does not like reading and avoids it, but she surprises herself by enjoying novels that are read to her. However, she needs much explaining to keep the story in her head.

Brooke has difficulty understanding newspaper articles that she is required to use for her work in several subjects.

She has little confidence in her written work. Whether she has to write a short-answer response or a longer piece, she finds that she simply cannot make a start and sits for a long time without beginning. Written analysis is very difficult.

Brooke has trouble grasping what she is supposed to do from instructions in her work booklets. She is uncertain about her work and asks for reassurance often.

Brooke worries about her future and is keen to get a part-time job.

Despite her difficulties, Brooke is always very pleasant in manner.

any LLD students have difficulty generating vocabulary and
can cause difficulties in getting started on the research process.
prevent their feeling overwhelmed by the task, it is important to
ld up skills slowly. There are additional steps that can be added
re students confront text.

PLANNING
REASONING
REFLECTING

meaning of words
limited vocabulary

CHAPTER 3

Adolescence and LLD – a Potent Mix

Early adolescence and the transition to secondary school

There is no single path through adolescence to adulthood. There is much trial and error. Some choices lead to a dead end and adolescents must retrace their steps and try a new way. The interaction of rapid pubescent growth, emotional and cognitive development, and family and social expectations becomes more complex. Change lacks the steady, continuous stream of primary school.

Emotional transition

As well as having to cope with a major transition from primary school, adolescents have to deal with their growing and changing bodies. Through this awareness of bodily change, adolescents also become aware of their individual strengths and weaknesses, and focus more intensely on questions such as:

- Who am I? (that is, the question of self-concept); and
- How do I feel about myself? (that is, the question of self-esteem).

In this time of change and self-examination, adolescents can often become confused about their goals and distinctiveness, and worry about whether they are outside the norm. There is intense evaluation of their abilities in relation to their peers in the secondary environment – which is less personal than the primary school environment. This can be a particularly demanding time for LLD students because of their additional difficulties in coping with the secondary school curriculum. The negative effect on the self-concept of students who perceive that they have a problem means that some find difficulty in resolving identity issues and in making even the most elementary decisions.

Several factors markedly affect this stage of development and transition.

- In the early years of secondary school, students with LLD are very vulnerable. The marked drop in self-esteem that occurs in these years can be particularly devastating to them and very difficult to repair in later school years.
- In the case of *boys*, persistent behaviour problems in the areas of 'attention, concentration, distractibility, persistence, compliance and general self-regulation

of behaviour' (Prior *et al.*, 1983–2000, p. 41), combined with poor reading and continuing weak phonological skills have been identified in adolescents who are at risk at the end of primary school.

- With respect to *girls*, apart from the obvious reading and weak phonological skills, underlying language problems are implicated in continuing learning difficulties at the end of primary school, although underlying language problems are suspected (Prior *et al.*, 1983–2000). The psychology of young teenage girls and their particular cultural and social problems might also place them at risk for a drop in self-esteem and require further study (Pipher, 1996).

- LLD students do not want to appear different from their peers and are therefore often reluctant to accept assistance or use equipment that will help them.

- Students with LLD might develop a range of avoidance behaviours to deny or cover their difficulties. If allowed to continue in the early years at secondary school, this behaviour can cause them to fall further behind academically, thus compounding their problems of self-esteem.

- They can perceive problems in extremes. For example, a student with LLD might announce: 'I can't read and I'm never going to be able to read'. This tendency to extreme views makes them vulnerable to depression and to extremely negative views of their chances of success. Alternatively, some students will go to the opposite extreme and have an unrealistically optimistic view of their chances of success.

- Given their emotional stage of development, they can be quick to blame others – rather than develop the self-understanding that is necessary for confronting their problems. This is a developmental stage they will need help to move through.

Cognitive development

Adolescents move into a phase of cognitive growth called the 'formal operational stage' which allows abstract thought, hypothetical–deductive reasoning, and more sophisticated thinking than was possible at earlier stages of development. Adolescents have a growing ability to:

- think about their own thinking;
- consider events removed in time and space;
- consider events real and imagined;
- consider all possible alternatives to problems and situations; and
- formulate and test hypotheses.

Secondary curriculum demands a high level of formal operational thought, but many adolescents find it difficult to function at a formal operational level of thought on a consistent basis. Thus there is often a mismatch between curriculum and capacity. This increases the likelihood of lack of success and alienation at a critical time when students' sense of identity is forming and is crucial to future development.

For LLD students the following are of particular note.

- They often have a very limited understanding of their problems.
- They don't know what they don't know – asking questions and self-monitoring are therefore difficult.
- Their skill base is low and is often insufficient to meet the reading, writing and oral language demands of the secondary curriculum without support, modification of the curriculum and, in some cases, direct instruction in skills (such as reading and reading comprehension).
- They do not retain skills (for example, dictionary skills and keyboard skills) that have been carefully taught at primary school unless they continue to practise them. It is important that skill development is carefully monitored throughout these early years so that students do not arrive in the later grades poorly prepared.

Realignment of family relationships

In secondary school the role of parents and the influence of the family change. Sound communication skills are essential because adolescents need to be able to explore their options and talk through their situations. Limitations in communication prove a severe handicap here.

Given that LLD students cannot 'read between the lines' in conversations, they are unlikely to absorb subtle messages or hints. Conversations about work and expectations of school and family need to be direct and simple. LLD students might need to have information repeated and their comprehension checked. The challenge for parents is to make their conversations direct while being supportive and encouraging.

During adolescence, there is a move to greater reliance on peers and friends for support, mutual understanding and intimacy. LLD students can misunderstand situations at school, can become the butt of jokes and can suffer many other relationship problems during these critical years.

CHAPTER 4

Social Skills and Language

Pragmatics or social language

Social skills are important for adolescents, and social competence in adolescence is often an indication of success in later life. Limited social ability becomes increasingly obvious in adolescence and is difficult to change.

Communication requires the integration of verbal, nonverbal and implied messages as well as the use of colloquial and peer-group language. The social use of language is called *pragmatics*.

Social language includes using appropriate body language and facial expressions and the use of language that is suitable for the listener. The language used in conversation with a mate differs from the language used in conversation with the school principal. Social language also includes spontaneous conversation and the daily banter among peers.

The *rules of conversation* require that conversation must be coherent, that turns must be taken, that the speaker must give enough information for the listener to understand and respond and that the speaker must monitor the comprehension of the listener by noting reactions and responses.

The pragmatics of language use is a most important area of linguistic growth during the school years. As children develop awareness of others and become more expert in expressing themselves, they develop awareness of the listener's point of view and can adapt what they are saying to different situations and requirements.

Skills required

What skills do adolescents require to be able to juggle their communication to suit all circumstances?

- They need the ability to attend to, and to follow, logical conversation. Once a child reaches the age of 11, topics of conversation tend to become more abstract – talking about things in the past or what might happen in the future.

- They need to be able to make follow-on statements spontaneously – for example: 'Yeah, I saw that movie too'.

- They must be able to solve problems, work out solutions and give opinions with reasons. In doing so, they must be able to keep on a topic.
- They must know the 'lingo' of their peers. This is a changing and subtle language. For those who find language difficult, adjusting to different styles of talk is difficult, confusing and often embarrassing.
- They require knowledge of general conversational topics, and to be able to make choices and give preferences (for example, about football teams).
- They must be able to master polite forms in making requests – for example: 'I wonder if it would suit you to . . .?'; 'Would it be possible for me to . . .?'.
- They require the ability to express feelings and frustrations through appropriate language.
- They need to use social niceties and 'small talk' to create a positive impression – for example, saying 'good morning' and 'good bye' while maintaining eye contact.
- They must learn and practise social skills such as answering the telephone.
- To participate in classroom activities, they need to learn to use the formal language of the classroom. In the classroom, it is necessary to be able to process information quickly and efficiently. Misunderstandings are common for LLD students. These can be embarrassing and socially damaging. Students need to be able to express themselves lucidly and promptly if they are to participate in class discussion. If they do not have these skills, they leave themselves open to ridicule when they attempt to contribute to discussions because their comments are often inappropriate or mistimed.

Some common problems

Students who are socially inept are rarely popular and are often rejected, particularly outside the organised classroom.

1. With other students

Students with LLD can be the subject of bullying. This is often distressing, but sometimes they might not realise that certain comments are teasing or mean.

They might crave social acceptance by their peers but lack the skills and understanding to achieve this. This can result in such students being alone or on the edge of the group. They might seek to interact with adults or younger children.

Students with LLD can have difficulty expressing frustration and behave inappropriately. They can be impulsive and have no idea of the consequences. They can be inappropriately aggressive or passive and have no idea why they are rejected. They might not share and then wonder why others will not be friends.

They can be shy and awkward and described as 'odd'. This might be a result of their being unable to converse, or unable even to work out the rules of conversation.

Such rules are rarely taught, but seem to evolve. LLD students might therefore:

- interrupt often, without waiting to listen to answers;
- not mention the topic they are talking about;
- change topic suddenly; or
- talk on more than one topic at once.

This failure to understand and observe the 'unspoken rules' of conversation can make it difficult for the listener to get the message.

Ideas to help

Card games or board games with rules can teach skills in taking turns. Students might need to be taught to keep on a topic during conversation. If their behaviour is unusual and socially inappropriate, they might need to develop strategies to help them blend in with their peers. Discussion of comics that depict everyday interaction between people can be useful, although the subtleties of these everyday interactions can be difficult for students with LLD to work out.

2. In the classroom

Students with LLD might not appreciate the difference required in language when talking to teachers, as compared with talking to friends. They might have poor awareness of body language, vocabulary and tone of voice. They might be unaware that they are perceived as being rude.

They can be vague and non-specific and not realise that they are not making sense.

Students might be unable to ask questions appropriately. They might not understand what they are supposed to do. Indeed, they might not even realise that they do not understand.

They often find generalising difficult and so do not realise that they can make similar comments (or ask similar questions) on topics that are different, but related.

They can be slow to respond and might appear to be 'deaf'. They will not respond to sarcasm and they take comments literally.

Ideas to help

Students with LLD need feedback. They might need an adult to help monitor and explain what they are doing wrong.

Sometimes they need to be shown (rather then told) that their conversational tone and style is inappropriate. For example, imitating and exaggerating certain behaviour might help them to see that the tone in which they demanded an extension for an assignment negated the fact that they had said 'please'. But such mimicry and exaggeration must be handled with sensitivity and care.

They need to learn and practise skills through role play and rehearsal. This is necessary to help develop the language and social skills required for social interaction with peers, for work experience, for interviews and for a range of classroom interaction. They will need to practise conversations and think about responses to questions. For example, they could be asked:

- 'What would you say if you needed to request an extension for this assignment?';
- 'What would you say if you were seeking permission to change a sport?'; or
- 'What would you say if you wanted to make a complaint?'.

Teaching the basic skills of conversation is necessary for some students. These include the skills of staying on a topic, taking turns, being aware of the listener and learning appropriate ways of talking with different people. It is important that teachers are aware that the lack of skills in this area can make a difference for students in their relationships with other students. Indeed, assistance in such social skills can be of importance in all aspects of the student's life.

Staff might need to make a regular time to speak to individual students to ensure that they have an opportunity to signal that they are encountering social difficulties.

Teachers need to know that LLD students might not be able to do certain activities. For example, they might have difficulty giving unprepared answers or talks, or reading in front of the class. Being asked to do tasks of this sort can result in extreme distress or inappropriate behaviour.

PART 2

Teaching the Language Learning Disabled Student

ny LLD students have difficulty generating vocabulary and
can cause difficulties in getting started on the research process.
prevent their feeling overwhelmed by the task, it is important to
d up skills slowly. There are additional steps that can be added
re students confront text.

language

limited vocabulary • meaning of words

PLANNING
REASONING
REFLECTING

CHAPTER 5

Organisation for Independence at School

The challenge of secondary school

By the time that they reach secondary school, students are expected to be responsible for their own organisation and learning. To achieve this they will have to organise themselves to follow the timetable, move around the school, handle the increased homework expectations and cope with a much greater range of activities than they have previously experienced. This is a challenge for all students, but is especially difficult for those with language learning disabilities. These students often have faulty organisational techniques. Moreover, they tend to use them rigidly and persistently, demonstrating an inertia when encouraged to change these unsatisfactory habits. By looking at the areas of organisation required, teachers can help put strategies in place to facilitate planning of tasks and thus minimise what often seems to be chaos for these students.

Class teachers need to be well prepared to assist LLD students so that organisation can be reinforced. Although teachers might feel that students can (and should) organise themselves, this is frequently not the case. For example, such apparently straightforward organisational tasks as writing homework into diaries and organising folders can be beyond these students. In first and second years, teachers must establish routines for doing these things. Such routines must be vigilantly checked to ensure that the practice is maintained and that a solid pattern is developed.

Organisation needs to be taught

Organisation is like an extra subject area – it needs to be taught. Learning to be organised is a critical skill that must be directly and relentlessly taught and reinforced if students are to become independent and in control of their own learning.

Within the school, students must:

- know how to read a timetable;
- know that timetables are flexible and might be altered;
- recall special arrangements or timetable changes – arrangements that might be made days or even weeks ahead;

- understand the meaning of bells;

- respond to notices read over loudspeakers or read from bulletins;

- be prepared for changes of teachers and different styles of teaching;

- be aware of the books that they have and what subjects they are used for;

- arrive at class on time with the books and equipment required for that class;

- select the number of books to be carried for subjects (and not to overload themselves by taking all books in case they are needed); and

- keep their lockers in reasonable order with a timetable inside for reference.

> Because he could not decide what he would need, Tom carried:
> - all the books his mother had bought him for English and Maths;
> - his computer;
> - a large pencil case; and
> - an extra folder with paper and slip-in pockets.
>
> This load weighed him down, made him look different and resulted in his coming late for nearly every class. In addition, once he arrived in class, he spent excessive time looking through his things for what he needed. The books took up all the space on his desk and all around him.

Strategies to support independence at school

Teachers and other support staff can help students become more independent at school by implementing a number of simple strategies.

Materials and folders

It is common for secondary students to use folders for subjects. To use these effectively, students must be systematic and organised.

They must:

- use the correct folder for each subject and not reach for the nearest folder (thus ending up with work from different subjects randomly spread through a selection of folders);

- have a sufficient supply of paper and plastic pockets to store assignments and notes;

- group together the pages from one unit of work;

- be able to maintain folders in order, using dividers to arrange material appropriately according to subject, or topic, or date; sometimes books with numbered pages are preferable to loose sheets of paper; and

- regularly tidy up their files and sort their work, removing (and storing) completed work at the end of term.

Toby had such a disorganised mess within his folders that a whole period was spent trying to find the parts of an assignment that he had completed. When the various pieces of work were found and organised, he discovered that he had actually started the assignment three times with different helpers who had each been unaware of what had been done before.

Staff with a particular interest in helping students with LLD can assist in the following ways.

Help from colleagues

Teachers can ask colleagues to list books and equipment required on specific days, and arrange for these to be listed inside students' locker doors. Teachers can have backup textbooks and other materials for times when students are not properly prepared.

Lockers

As well as assisting students by listing books and equipment inside students' lockers, teachers can also help students who might need assistance in organising their lockers.

Folders

Teachers can actively assist students to maintain well-organised folders. Colour-coding spines of students' books and folders according to subject can help. Folders need to kept up to date with subject and topic pages filed together. Students should be encouraged to date pages.

Expanding files

Expanding files can be easier to manage than folders. These folders can have each section allocated to a subject, and labelled accordingly. All current work for that subject is kept in the appropriate section. One section is kept for paper supplies.

By using an expanding file, students need take only their expanding file (and textbooks) to class, thus saving the trouble of locating and bringing appropriate individual folders. Work is removed from the expanding file when finished and placed into folders. If it is decided that an expanding file is a good idea for a particular student, time needs to be set aside to organise this with him or her.

Diaries

Diaries or record books are essential for personal organisation. Students must:

- carry diaries all the time;
- have a personal timetable within them, checked for accuracy in all details;
- record arrangements;
- write all the details of homework including the due date, with items being ticked off when the work is completed; and
- list special requirements or equipment to be brought to school.

A routine of checking that the details in the diary are correct might need to be instituted until such a strategy becomes automatic. This process can take an extended time to establish.

Timetables

School timetables are often extremely complicated and subject to change. Students need explicit instruction to ensure that they find their way to the right place at the right time. The following might help to make this a little easier.

- Teachers should ensure that students have an accurate timetable in their diaries. Copying the timetable into diaries as a whole class activity is too difficult for many LLD students; it needs to be individually checked.

- Teachers should check that the students know how to read a timetable and that they understand all abbreviations (such as 'LOTE', 'Phys Ed', 'IT', and so on).

- Students should always carry timetables. Teachers should have a master timetable with them to sort out any confusion on the spot if needed.

- Students should keep a timetable at home for reference. This should have a list of equipment needed each day (for example, sports equipment or musical instruments). The timetable should be kept in a convenient and prominent place at home for easy consultation by students and family members (who can thus assist with reminders as needed).

- Teachers should ensure that students know where noticeboards and clocks are so that they can be independent about clarifying information and times.

Essential organisation techniques

Teachers and students

It is important for students to be organised in their senior years at secondary school, but this is a skill that takes years to learn. For students with LLD it is vital that organisational skills be taught from first year. LLD students need to make conscious efforts to become organised. They must recognise that this is an area in which they have problems and they must be constantly reminded to attend to the organisation of themselves, their books, their diaries and their assignments. Constant reinforcement from teaching staff can help to make such organisation easier for these students.

Here are some general strategies which can help students and teachers in this regard.

Peer-support network

Provide a peer-support network. This provides good models and non-threatening people with whom to check arrangements and details (for example, 'When do we have to finish this page?').

Bringing materials to school

Parents, teachers and students should attempt to ensure that students put record books, disks, schoolwork and other materials back into schoolbags after doing homework. Even if the students do not believe that this work is required at school next day, they should not leave these materials at home. This avoids problems that arise when students misread the timetable and find that they do need these materials after all.

Follow-up of homework not done

Homework that is not completed should be followed up immediately. At the start of secondary school it is useful to follow up by phoning students' parents to let them know. It is not sufficient merely to give no grade on a report for homework that is not completed. This does not teach students to become better organised and is an ineffective strategy.

Forewarning

Forewarn students individually about upcoming events, assignments, duties and activities. Do not expect that they will necessarily take in information that is given to the class as a whole. Alert them individually to information that is relevant to them.

Parental involvement

Many parents are eager to help their children to succeed. A good relationship between parents and the school can make life easier for everyone, and should be encouraged. Apart from the aspects of parental involvement already noted above, the following should be kept in mind.

Communication with parents

Teachers should institute a communication system with parents via a diary, or by telephone or e-mail, to clarify issues and requirements.

Requirements and expectations

There needs to be contact with parents early in the year to discuss requirements and expectations. This will help alleviate anxiety and unnecessary pressure on teachers and students.

The importance of learning to be organised

Learning to be organised is fundamental to many other life skills. Although learning problems are likely to continue in one form or another, *learning to be organised* ensures that students make the most of their abilities and the learning opportunities that are available. Directly teaching and monitoring organisational strategies is certainly worthwhile. The benefits to students are enormous.

Year-level guide

The following table traces the key skills that teachers should try to tackle as students move through school. It outlines some of the developmental milestones that are important to achieve if students are to have the best possible chance of success at school and beyond.

Table 5.1 Behavioural and social issues

Secondary years 1–2	Secondary years 3–4	Secondary years 5–6
Important to identify problems early on (if possible before transition to secondary school).		
Students begin to develop understanding of their strengths and weaknesses. Learn to accept help and modification.	Students able to identify strengths and areas of difficulty. Use appropriate strategies for dealing with difficulties. Must still be prepared to accept assistance and modifications to work.	Appropriate selection of courses (with majority of work in strength areas). Prepared to accept help and modification in areas of weakness. (Sixth year demands and arrangements might preclude this.)
Introduce strategies to assist learning.	Further develop strategies to assist learning and independence.	Self-monitoring. Actively seek assistance with specific problems. (Students who cannot identify areas of strength and weakness find fifth and sixth years difficult.)
Begin to reflect on work. Recognise a need to be able to identify strengths and weaknesses.	Realistic assessment of options for fifth and sixth years might reveal need to take a different path to peers. Anxiety about the future can arise earlier for LLD students than for peers (who might stay in same environment until end of sixth year). Actively encourage discussion of possible pathways. Develop self-monitoring.	Students need to consider all alternatives and options. Students becoming largely independent but might need help organising notes for study. At this level, studying and exam strategies are required. Students might need to consider all alternatives and options.
A difficult time. Students perhaps angry, or perhaps deny any learning difficulty. Vulnerable to poor self-esteem and less confidence. Avoidance behaviour should be identified. Coaching in social skills very valuable.	Continue work on social skills.	Require increased assistance in prioritising work (helps to avoid panic in times of stress). Help might be needed to accept constructive criticism.

Table 5.2 Skill development

Secondary years 1–2	Secondary years 3–4	Secondary years 5–6
Revisit reading (gains can continue with assistance). Use bypass techniques to make reading less daunting. Reduce amount and complexity of reading tasks. Use books on tape. Student comprehension needs to be carefully checked.	Continue with reading skills. Continue use of bypass techniques. Continue to check comprehension.	Might still need assistance with reading. Focus on reading comprehension (rather than mechanics of reading). Listening to texts on tape useful. Never too late to learn to read (but not realistic for general classroom teachers to do this in senior years).
Intensive spelling and transfer of spelling skills into writing.	Continue intensive spelling and transfer of spelling into writing.	Marked improvement still possible at this level. One-to-one assistance perhaps needed.
Constant check of skills needed for classroom. High level of monitoring and immediate feedback on learning. Feedback best done one-to-one (avoids embarrassment). Support students through preteaching program (see 'Preteaching', Chapter 6).	Continue constant monitoring of skills. Preteaching still helpful.	Preteaching can still be helpful in senior years.

Table 5.3 Curriculum skills

Secondary years 1–2	Secondary years 3–4	Secondary years 5–6
Direct structured teaching of writing in conjunction with reading and spelling plans.	Development of plans in key writing areas: narratives; argumentative; compare & contrast; analytical; persuasive; etc. (LLD students need eight practices of each plan; non-LLD students need only two.)	Strong focus on writing using plans developed from the start of secondary school.
Preteaching, especially vocabulary, novels, texts, maths, science (see 'Preteaching', Chapter 6, page 32).	Preteaching still valuable. Vocabulary more complex.	Vocabulary development continues. Language more complex.
Teaching organisational skills as part of each subject.	Continue reinforcing organisational skills.	Work on organisation for studying.
Individual and small group sessions. Work in these sessions based on curriculum.	Continue small group sessions.	Small group sessions still useful.
Develop writing portfolio.	Continue developing writing portfolio.	
Need to look at amount of work and time allocation. Vital to give students tasks they are able to finish – a great boost to self-esteem. Learning to complete tasks is important.	Focus on completing tasks.	Students who have not learned to complete tasks will find fifth and sixth years difficult.
Specific targeted instruction before general classroom instruction.	Targeted instruction still valuable.	Targeted instruction still valuable for senior students.
Monitor progress of tasks. Use criterion sheets. (See 'How to Modify the Amount of Work', Chapter 13.)		

Table 5.4 Looking to the future

Secondary years 1–2	Secondary years 3–4	Secondary years 5–6
Establish good working habits by end of second year.	If literacy remains a major difficulty, will need to look carefully at Year 12 alternatives.	Self-monitoring and organisation continues to be an issue.
Intensive spelling and transfer of spelling skills into writing.	Work experience: LLD students need considerable preparation for this.	Work experience.

Students have difficulty generating vocabulary and can cause difficulties in getting started on the research process. To prevent their feeling overwhelmed by the task, it is important to build up skills slowly. There are additional steps that can be added before students confront text.

CHAPTER 6

Preteaching

Need for preteaching

Students with LLD benefit from preteaching before being introduced to new topics in class. These students often make poor progress in maths and reading in large groups. The reality is that one teacher with thirty students will not have the time to work through important processes, such as editing, at a pace needed by students with LLD. It is difficult to cater for individual needs (for detailed, intensive instruction) in bigger classes where teachers have a large amount of content to work through.

Some techniques that are helpful for LLD students are difficult to apply in general classrooms because they are either unsuitable for non-LLD students or would embarrass LLD students if used in front of their peers. Some strategies help LLD students but can slow down other students. For example, self-questioning strategies to improve the reading comprehension of LLD students might actually lower the reading comprehension of students without disabilities (Wong & Jones, 1982; Swanson, Cooney & Overholser, 1989).

What is preteaching?

Preteaching does not replace general classroom teaching and nor does it duplicate what will be covered in class. The general classroom teacher provides the curriculum content whereas the person taking the preteaching session looks at the detailed strategies and knowledge required by students to link into the mainstream curriculum.

Preteaching classes might:
- introduce vocabulary;
- develop questioning skills;
- explain ideas and major concepts;
- develop notetaking to improve comprehension and identify keywords and themes;
- assist students to connect new knowledge to existing knowledge;
- outline story sequences, develop chapter and story summaries and make character lists that provide a basis for classroom work on novels;
- develop concept maps to aid memory of key ideas and new vocabulary;

- explain forthcoming assignments and tests and the procedures required (for example: 'Next week you are going to be given this assignment and you will have to do the following . . . '); and
- involve 'mock' tests in a similar format to the real thing.

Small group or individual classes are better *before* the general classroom lesson for a number of reasons. In particular, LLD students cope far better in class when pretaught topics are later introduced. Students are confident, rather than confused.

Without preteaching, LLD students come to a general class with poorly developed word knowledge. These students become lost at the beginning of a lesson because they spend so much time decoding new words and are unable to concentrate on comprehension. In contrast, in a preteaching class, the language of the new topic can be presented at a slower pace. Students can be questioned to clarify that they know the vocabulary and that they have made connections with prior knowledge. This helps them store and access information better from memory. When the teacher introduces the new topic in a general class, LLD students will have some prior knowledge of the language and be able to concentrate on comprehension of the teacher's instructions.

All students benefit when teachers include a discussion of the vocabulary to be used to help them make connections with previous knowledge. However, time constraints often mean that the presentation of this information in general classrooms is too rapid for LLD students. This is particularly so if students are hearing the information for the first time. They might need to hear key information more than once. The preteaching class can allow for this, giving LLD students the benefit of having the information reinforced and extended in the general classroom.

Once students have made errors in comprehension, the task of *reteaching* them is much more difficult and time-consuming. Preteaching maximises the opportunities for students to get the information correct in the first place.

This checking of comprehension goes beyond the classroom technique of reading a passage, discussing it and then answering questions. Preteaching before a general lesson makes sure that the basic comprehension of students is correct and helps them to obtain the most from the general classroom lesson – for example, by ensuring that students can remember the names of the characters in a novel, or that students have an accurate visual image to go with the words on the page. Most LLD students need considerable preparation before they can join in tasks like this in groups with their peers – especially with more complex novels such as *To Kill a Mockingbird* or plays such as *Macbeth*.

Preteaching is a boost to the *confidence* of LLD students and helps them to present as capably as possible in front of their peers. Given the considerable loss in self-esteem that LLD adolescents suffer, such confidence is important. Preteaching is an excellent way of maximising positive learning experiences in the normal classroom.

Requirements for preteaching

Rather than being an 'extra' before or after school, preteaching should, if possible, be part of the school day. To provide time for preteaching, LLD students might need to take fewer subjects at any given Year level. Doing more things is not necessarily the answer. Instead, it is better to allow time for direct teaching if students are to complete major curriculum tasks competently. This builds better skills and enhances self-esteem.

Preteaching requires team teaching involving the general classroom teacher, the curriculum support coordinator and the person conducting the preteaching classes. A curriculum support coordinator is necessary – given the number of teachers in a typical secondary school and the extent of the curriculum to be covered in preteaching classes. With sufficient forward planning, the curriculum support coordinator can ensure that preteaching classes are provided for novels, assignments and vocabulary several weeks in advance, and can ensure that those working with LLD students are aware of individual progress and learning. This is especially important if the preteaching sessions for individuals and small groups are conducted by school consultants such as speech language pathologists, psychologists, and special education teachers. These people need this coordinating information if they are to make the content of their sessions relevant to students.

In an ideal situation the curriculum support might be organised as shown in Figure 6.1. The details in various schools might differ, but the important feature is that the curriculum support coordinator should communicate with *all* parties to ensure the best educational outcomes for students.

Figure 6.1 Structure of curriculum support staff

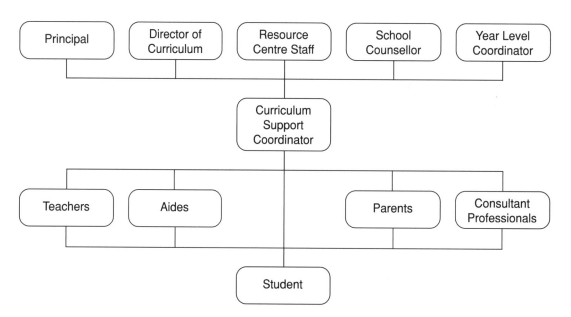

Mandy Brent, Florence Gough, Susan Robinson

Clear communication and cooperation among all involved parties is vital. Respect for the individual skills that each member of the teaching team brings to the task of assisting LLD students is also vital. It is important that each member of the teaching team understands that the input of others is necessary if the work is to be carried out effectively.

> Phoebe had enormous difficulty in her maths classes. She was never able to answer questions and had become very anxious about maths.
>
> Before she began the next new topic, her classroom teacher arranged for Phoebe to have some extra time on the new concepts, vocabulary and processes that would be taught. In these preteaching classes Phoebe had one-to-one help with the basics of the new topic. Her classroom teacher was delighted to see that Phoebe's confidence in her maths had improved to such a degree that Phoebe was even raising her hand in class to answer questions!

A final thought on preteaching

Superficially, it might seem that preteaching is merely teaching LLD students the same things twice. In reality, it is much more than that. Preteaching offers LLD students the opportunity to make the most of their time in the general classroom and gives them the best chance to succeed. It often has the added benefit of increasing the participation and confidence of students.

any LLD students have difficulty generating vocabulary and
can cause difficulties in getting started on the research process.
prevent their feeling overwhelmed by the task, it is important to
ld up skills slowly. There are additional steps that can be added
re students confront text.

PLANNING
REASONING
REFLECTING

CHAPTER **7**

Reading

Decoding and comprehension

Reading usually poses enormous problems for LLD students. Virtually all LLD students have significant difficulty with one or more aspects of reading. Young children who have a history of difficulty with oral language often go on to become students with reading difficulties after they have started school (Tallal 1988). There are other students, whose oral language appears to be normal, who also have difficulty learning to read.

In the majority of cases, reading disability is described as a language disability. Research on this topic is very extensive and we now have a very clear picture of the factors involved in oral and written language difficulties and of the factors that are important in effective intervention strategies.

Reading is a complex set of skills but, for the purposes of this chapter, reading involves the processes of:

- decoding – word identification and dealing effectively with the code of written language; and
- comprehension – understanding what has been decoded.

The purpose of reading is to *comprehend* the information presented, and the *decoding* of words, on its own, is therefore not enough to constitute competent reading. But students who struggle to identify words must put so much conscious effort and mental attention into that part of the process that they cannot put their minds to the task of *understanding* what they read. Until decoding is accurate, fluent and automatic, students cannot 'multitask' – that is, they cannot do more than one thing at a time. They cannot focus on meaning and decoding simultaneously. Decoding needs to be automatic for proficient reading. Reading involves both decoding *and* comprehension.

Reading and the LLD student

By the time that they reach secondary school, what is the picture for LLD students? For many, there has been a long struggle to learn word identification (decoding) skills and, despite their own efforts and the efforts of parents and teachers, it is common for these students to remain halting readers who do not recognise words quickly or fluently. Some develop a level of reading proficiency that allows them to read some material, while still being unable to master the complex wording contained in the texts and novels they need to read at secondary level.

Others develop some skill in decoding text, but remain slow and make many mistakes. By the time that they reach secondary school, these students have experienced so much frustration and lack of reward for their efforts that they do not find the task enjoyable and they do not find what they read interesting. They do not want to spend any more of their time on it. They are reluctant to read, but they are reluctant with very good reason! Others are more than reluctant and become determined to avoid reading at all costs.

Some students decode words well but have difficulty with comprehending what they are reading. This is sometimes referred to as 'barking at print'. Although the method used to teach students to read is frequently blamed, this difficulty is usually part of a wider difficulty with language comprehension. Language comprehension difficulties can be obvious, but they can also be quite subtle and still make a huge impact on students' performances at school.

Other students might decode reasonably well but have difficulty comprehending what they read because of the way that different forms of reading are structured.

Common types of classroom texts

Narratives

Narratives are often easy to read and, in primary school, are the most common style of books presented. Although narratives are generally approachable, they can be complex – especially at the secondary level. The story might not follow a chronological sequence, but can move back and forth in time with no explanation and no helpful linking statements. Characters can be involved simultaneously with internal thoughts and external events. This switching of internal thought and external event might be implicit and not made explicit. For example in John Marsden's *So Much to Tell You*, past and present must be deduced from personal diary entries. In Julie Ireland's *A Kind of Dreaming* there are different characters who lived at different times in history, but gradually merge. This merging is shown by the use of a different font.

Several themes can run simultaneously and be intertwined. This can be confusing. The connections between events are implied and not stated. These connections need to be made explicit for students with reading difficulties.

For example:

> As we walked up the sidewalk, we saw a solitary light burning in the distance.
> 'That's funny,' said Jem, 'jail doesn't have an outside light.'
> 'Looks like it's over the door,' said Dill.
> A long extension cord ran between the bars of a second-floor window and down the side of the building. In the light from its bare bulb, Atticus was sitting propped against the front door. He was sitting in one of his office chairs, and he was reading, oblivious of the night bugs dancing over his head.
>
> Harper Lee
> *To Kill a Mockingbird*

On reading the passage above, Nathan, a third year student, was amazed to discover that Atticus was sitting outside.

'Why didn't they just say that?' he asked.

He had missed all the cues in the text. The connection needed to be made explicit for him to understand the action.

Comprehension often relies on a great deal of 'world knowledge' – a broad knowledge of events, people, and references. LLD students are not good at picking up what is going on around them and are often unaware of things that are common knowledge. Literary references can thus be extremely confusing, as shown in the following portion of text.

> Breakfast over, Aunt Polly had family worship; it began with a prayer built from the ground up of solid courses of scriptural quotations wedded together with a thin mortar of originality; as from the summit of this she delivered a grim chapter of the Mosaic Law, as from Sinai.
>
> Mark Twain
> *The Adventures of Tom Sawyer*

The above extract relies on the reader having prior knowledge of the Bible. This connection would need to be made explicit to LLD students if they are to understand the passage.

Students with LLD often have difficulties making connections between items appearing in a text.

> The key snagged briefly as he slid it into the lock. As he pushed the door open and stepped into the hall, Barney sensed desolation. He did not call 'I'm home!'. There was no one there to answer. He felt it. He let the dog in, hung up his bags and sat at the table to think. He stood the empty whisky bottle upright and then he stood and walked slowly through the house, looking into each room. She was home! There in the bath, her head on one side, her hand resting on her leg. White tinged with purple was how he would describe her colour. Hanging from its cord and lying at the bottom of the bath was the grey shape of her hairdryer. 'Goodbye, Barney. Have a good life,' she had said as he slammed the front door that morning.
>
> Florence Gough

For students with LLD to comprehend this passage they would have to make many connections: the hairdryer in the bath, the colour of her skin, and the meaning behind her parting comments in the morning. It is quite possible that students with learning difficulties will not have made the necessary connections to conclude that suicide had occurred.

Textbooks

Textbooks are often complex and difficult for students with LLD. The vocabulary is subject-specific and is often language that is not commonly used or heard by students outside the study of the subject. Indeed, the vocabulary might be entirely new to students.

Sentences are often tightly worded and use complex sentence structure. There are often many clauses that make the passages difficult to 'unpack'. Students with LLD might not be able to form such sentences themselves, and often cannot understand this formal, detailed style of language when they encounter it. Consider the following example:

- Factories often discharge their polluted water directly into rivers or the sea.
- The storm water system which is designed to carry away rainwater from roads and houses often picks up a variety of pollutants before it drains into a river or sea.
- Excess fertilisers or pesticides are often washed from farms into rivers . . . Not only can human activity add pollutants to the river, it can also alter such things as the temperature and the amount of oxygen.

Malcolm Parsons
Heinemann Outcomes Science 2

As can be seen in the above example, information is often expressed concisely, with not a word being wasted. LLD students need such language expanded and reworded (preferably in everyday language) to be able to understand it. The above example could become:

- Factories sometimes produce wastes that can cause pollution. Water is often used to wash the wastes away. This water might flow from the factories straight into rivers or the sea.
- The stormwater system is made up of drains, which carry away the rainwater that falls on roads and houses. Stormwater often collects pollution before it runs to the sea.
- If too much fertiliser or spray is used on farms, this will also run into the rivers. People do lots of things that cause pollution. This pollution can also change the water temperature and the amount of oxygen there is.

How to assist

Assistance can be offered in the following ways.

A range of texts

Faculties should use a range of novels and texts of various levels of complexity. Select a range of novels – some with more straightforward storyline and themes than others.

Illustrations

Materials should have pictures and diagrams with small 'grabs' of text.

Layout

Small type is very daunting. Presenting a crowded dense page of print can ruin the confidence of LLD students before they even begin. Look for editions that use bigger print and spacious layout.

Abridged versions

Find abridged versions of novels. For example, *Readers' Digest* condensed books or other abridged versions are available. Some books use the same language as the original but reduce the length of the book by selecting sections. Others simplify the text. Both types of abridged novels can be useful.

Taped novels

Use taped novels. There is quite a range available now. When teachers are selecting novels they could bear in mind those that have tapes available. This information is available from audiotape catalogues. If taped novels are not commercially available, it might be possible to arrange suitable volunteers to read the novels. (For more on this subject, see 'Problems with taping' on page 43.)

Prepared summaries

Use prepared summaries of the books to give an outline. Reading the summary first gives an overview of the storyline and acts as a preteaching strategy. Providing such a context allows for better comprehension without the clutter of too much detail at first.

Two such summaries are shown in Figures 7.1 and 7.2. These examples show the level of detail that is required as well as highlighting some of the more difficult vocabulary in the text. Figure 7.1 illustrates such a summary for *Elli, Coming of Age in the Holocaust* (suitable for fourth year) and Figure 7.2 illustrates *A Little Princess*.

Character summaries

Character summaries and diagrams of relationships and events can help LLD students to understand characters and make connections between them as the plot unfolds.

Cartoons

Cartoons are often helpful. These can be quite simple and hand-drawn. Some are available commercially but can be complicated. Figure 7.3 shows a cartoon of *A Midsummer Night's Dream*. This illustrates that complex plots can be unpacked and presented in a simple way to help LLD students understand the intricacies.

'Post-it' stickers

Use 'post-it' stickers to summarise key events and characters in each chapter. Stick these in at the end of each chapter. These help students to remember what has happened and to keep track of the storyline. It also allows students to move back and forth through the book to find information. This is otherwise a difficult task for LLD students because skimming is difficult for them.

Figure 7.1 Prepared summary of *Elli, Coming of Age in the Holocaust*

	Elli, Coming of Age in the Holocaust by Livia Bitton Jackson	
	This story is told by a 13-year old Jewish girl who lives in Hungary in the town of Somorja.	
1	At the start, Elli enjoys a happy life with her family in the small country town of Somorja near the Carpathian Mountains. She is a keen student and hopes that she will be allowed to go to the capital city of Budapest to study at the secondary school like her brother, Bubi.	gymnasium = high school
2	The war has been on for some time and Hungary has been occupied by the Germans. Food is hard to find, and German propaganda, especially against the Jews, is frightening. Before the war, the family had owned a business, but this had been confiscated. Elli's father is becoming depressed, but tries not to show this. One night, the Hungarian military police visit. They search, and destroy things in the shop. They accuse Elli's father of illegal behaviour, and he is fined. One night Bubi comes back unexpectedly from Budapest. He says that the Germans have invaded Budapest. No one else seems to know about it although he saw the tanks and soldiers.	Elli, Ellike = various forms of the writer's name
3	Bubi is certain about his news but, since it is not confirmed by anyone else, his father sends him back to Budapest thinking it was a false alarm. As soon as he has returned, the news of the invasion is confirmed. The father wants to go and find Bubi, but it is too dangerous, and Bubi comes back to Somorja.	
4	Bubi manages to escape Budapest without being noticed because he is blond and blue-eyed. These are Aryan features that the Nazis do not consider to be Jewish. Everyone in Budapest is scared and the police search for Jews and arrest them, sometimes dragging them off the train.	Aryan = a race of people with blond hair and blue eyes that Hitler considered to be the perfect race
5	In Somorja, they feel safe and life goes on as normal for another week. But the Jews are worried. Suddenly schools are ordered closed (March 1944). On the way home from school that day, Elli is taunted by a group of schoolboys ('Hey, Jew girl! Jew girl!'). This is the beginning of the end of her life as she has known it.	
6	The Jews have to report to the town hall to be counted and tagged. They have to give up a lot of their possessions – jewellery, radios, bikes – including Elli's brand-new bike. There are feelings of helpless rage and humiliation. Elli's father buries the family's jewellery in the ground of the cellar so they can find it later when their lives have returned to normal. Jews are ordered to wear a yellow Star of David on their clothing. They are arrested if they do not wear one. Elli is humiliated and refuses to go outside, but Bubi tries to wear his badge with pride. He tells Elli that she is a coward because she does not want to be seen outside with the star on. He shames her into going to the school to receive her diploma.	
7	Jews are forbidden to have anything to do with non-Jews, and forbidden to go into public places. They are told that all Jews are to be taken to another town called Nagymagyar. They pack what they can on a cart, visit their grandparent's graves, give the keys of their house to the Hungarian police, and leave. Elli suffers stomach aches – the first of many that she is to suffer.	gentiles = non-Jews ghetto = a restricted area where people from the same race or lifestyle live *judenfrei* = German word for 'Jew-free'

Florence Gough

Figure 7.2 Prepared summary of *A Little Princess*

A Little Princess by Frances Hodgson Burnett	
Chapter 1 Sara	**Chapter 1 Vocabulary**
Sara Crewe, the main character, has just arrived in England with her father. Although Sara is English, she misses her life in India. While her father is away, Sara is going to live at Miss Minchin's Select Seminary for Young Ladies. Sara dislikes the seminary when she arrives. Before her father leaves her, they go shopping for clothes and a new doll.	Sara Crewe = the main character of the story seminary = school
Chapter 2 A French Lesson	**Chapter 2 Vocabulary**
Sara is having her first lesson. Her classmates are interested in her as she is new to the seminary. Miss Minchin tells Sara she must take French lessons. When the French teacher arrives, Sara explains to him in French that she already knows the French she was told to learn. Miss Minchin becomes embarrassed and starts to dislike Sara.	Miss Minchin = the principal of the seminary
Chapter 3 Ermengarde	**Chapter 3 Vocabulary**
Sara is in the classroom, sitting beside Miss Minchin. She notices a girl named Ermengarde St John. Ermengarde is not good at learning French. She is often laughed at by her classmates. Sara introduces herself to Ermengarde, and the two girls become friends. Sara takes Ermengarde to meet her new doll.	Ermengarde = a good friend of Sara's. She is generous and good-tempered.
Chapter 4 Lottie	**Chapter 4 Vocabulary**
Sara is talking to Ermengarde about everything that has happened to her (she thinks) by chance. They also talk about Lavinia, who is a spiteful girl in their class. The scene changes to Lavinia talking with her friend Jessie about Sara. Lavinia is jealous of Sara because of her wealth and her friendliness. The scene changes again to one day when Sara finds Lottie Legh screaming in the hallway. Lottie and Sara talk and they find out that they have one thing in common – neither of them has a mother.	Lottie Legh = one of the youngest girls who lives in the seminary Lavinia = one of the oldest girls at the seminary. She dislikes Sara because she is popular.

Prepared by a VCE student for Florence Gough

Figure 7.3 Cartoon and notes on *A Midsummer Night's Dream*

Florence Gough

Forward planning and liaison

Forward planning and liaison with faculties is essential. Find out in advance what students have to read.

LLD students generally do not read quickly, and often underestimate the time it will take them to read. It is a good strategy to 'get in first' and have LLD students begin on their reading before other students. Discuss the novel as students go along to retain interest in the storyline and to check that comprehension is accurate. Usually, students will require longer and more detailed explanations to grasp the information fully.

Problems with taping

Although audiotaping books is very helpful for LLD students, some words of caution are appropriate.

Permissions

If no commercial tapes are available, permission to tape published books must be sought from the publisher.

Time needed

Taping books takes a long time and volunteers cannot be expected to produce them 'overnight'. Forward planning is essential.

Reading skills

Readers must have suitable voices and be clear, careful readers who pay attention to detail. Readers need to read at a deliberate pace and in a way that captures interest.

With training, older students can perform this task well. Having a peer of a similar age reading the book onto tape is motivating for students who will hear the tape. It can benefit the reader if credits are available for community service requirements. If older students are assisting with this task, they require training and staff support to complete the task successfully.

Videotapes

Videotapes of novels can also be useful. But note that there can be significant differences between the book and the film.

Discuss the video with students with a view to helping with the storyline. Comprehension difficulties can affect their understanding of the plot. Students might not be able to analyse the film meaningfully until they have watched it several times.

Summary

It is never too late for students to learn to read. Given a positive attitude, students must be given every opportunity for direct instruction while they are at school. Realistically, this needs to be done outside the general classroom – with the option of individual instruction.

CHAPTER 8

Libraries and Research

Dealing with information

In all areas of the secondary curriculum, students are required to access information quickly from a variety of sources. This is difficult for students with LLD because they need considerably more structure and interaction with teachers to be able to gather appropriate information. Care must be taken to ensure that students understand the purpose of the activity so they can select suitable sources, and that they select sources containing material that they are able to read and understand.

Students with LLD commonly have difficulty with language comprehension. This limits the material they can use and limits the extent to which they can manage independently. For example, students might not be able to work out the main idea in a given piece of information without assistance.

Using technology with LLD students

Selecting technology

The most common equipment used with LLD students are computers, tape-recorders, calculators and word-processing packages with spell-checkers. Technology can be of great assistance to LLD students, but care needs to be taken when selecting the most appropriate equipment and software. It is important to remember the following points.

Individual differences

Individual differences significantly affect a student's ability to benefit from technology. What helps one student might hinder another. If possible, trial any equipment or software with a student before recommending its purchase.

Student reluctance

Some students will refuse to use technology that makes them appear to be different from their peers. Those students who benefit most from technology have faced up to the long-term nature of their disabilities and have a good understanding of their learning problems.

Learning and generalising

It might take some time for students to learn how to use the technology. In addition, students might need assistance in generalising skills already learned. That is, they might have difficulty in applying a learned skill to a new task – even if the new task employs similar strategies.

Technology not the complete answer

Technology might not make students completely independent. For example, it is difficult for LLD students to use a spell-checker. Their spelling might be very different from the target word and they might find it difficult to select the correct word from the options presented to them.

Word processors

Word-processing packages can help LLD students produce work more quickly and present a better end product by allowing resequencing and the easy correction of written errors. However, students still need considerable training to develop keyboard skills and still require teacher assistance with editing, spelling and grammatical errors. Research shows that discussion with the class teacher and redrafting is needed to improve the written language of LLD students (Wong, 1997).

Text-to-voice scanners

Text-to-voice scanners, originally designed for those with visual impairment, can be used to read a text. Voice quality on the technology is constantly being improved but currently lacks the depth and richness of the human voice. The text is read in a flat, synthesised monotone without appropriate inflection. This can prove difficult for some students to understand.

Text-to-voice scanners can be used to help students with poor silent-reading skills, but can decrease the performance of those students who have efficient silent reading.

One of the advantages of text-to-voice scanners is that the reading rate can be slowed as appropriate to the reader's progress. Although this distorts the voice quality, some students are able to use the cursor to follow the words and read along independently at a slower rate.

Libraries and databases

Collaboration with staff from resource centres or libraries is an effective means of teaching students (including LLD students) the skills required to access databases and other sources of information. The direct teaching of research skills fits well with the learning needs of LLD students and leads to less likelihood that students will be lost in the learning process. The skills and technology of database research need to be studied together.

The following ideas will assist in this dual process of collaborating effectively with resource staff and providing the discrete and sequential development needed by LLD students.

Liaison with staff

Make sure that resource centre staff are familiar with topic areas and receive copies of assignments and work requirements in advance.

Specify skills

Specify the skills needed and the steps in the process of acquiring the skill. In each lesson, include short periods (approximately fifteen minutes each) of specific skill activities. The simplest way is to add the skill to an existing task. For example, if a student already has a paragraph that has to be read, use this paragraph as a basis for a lesson (about fifteen minutes) on notetaking and the identification of keywords.

Specify content

Specify the precise content required in the final product. Prepare students for project work by providing a clear outline of the task content and the criteria for assessment. Teach students specific skills relevant to such content and assessments – such as the skill of notetaking, and the skill of distinguishing between non-fiction and fiction sources.

Skills needed to access information

Research skills are part of the process of learning to organise things. There are subsets of skills within each area. Teaching these skills is a big job and it cannot be done quickly or by using just one topic as a teaching example. It must be done over time – by both the classroom teacher and resource centre staff. This ensures that underprepared students are not overwhelmed and unskilled when they have to complete work requirements.

The old library catalogue system based on fixed criteria such as author, title, and subject heading has become obsolete. Now every word in the library catalogue sentence is searchable. Learning how to find things is an important skill.

Students need to learn how to:

- locate material;
- scan and extract information from located material;
- take notes;
- reconstruct the information; and
- present the information.

Locating Materials

What and where?

When using the library to research topics, students need to ask themselves questions such as: 'Where will I find things?' and 'Where will I start my research?'. To answer these questions, students must have a clear idea of what they need to know.

Students must look at the questions and assignments set by the class teacher and ask themselves exactly what they are being asked to do. They need to highlight any keywords. Understanding the question in this way helps to narrow the search.

What search words do these questions generate? Students can find a range of terms applying to those keywords under the catalogue system. They need to consider broader or narrower ways of exploring their topic. They need to ask if this is part of a bigger or smaller topic. Students should have a list of search terms by the end of the library session.

Through this teaching, students learn the skills of research and understand that it is not a linear process but, rather, a refining process as they search, read, gain more information, and narrow down their terms.

Handouts

Handouts are helpful for all students, and can be adapted to assist students with LLD. The following examples give an idea of what can be produced.

Handout 1

Keys to Researching a Topic

How do I get started?

The best way to begin is by brainstorming ideas and thoughts about your topic.

Ask yourself:

- What do I know?
- What do I need to find out?

An ideas map or 'mindmap' can be very useful at this stage. These maps can help you to see the connections between your thoughts and allows you to begin sorting these thoughts into related topics.

- Mindmaps can take many shapes The most common has branches coming out from a central title.
- Mindmaps are best on a rectangular page. This suits the way our eyes look across the page, and how our minds remember.
- Mindmaps are working documents. They should be refined and revised as you develop your topic.
- Mindmaps are best remembered when coloured pens and highlighters are used to show different ideas about the topic.

Figure 8.1 A mindmap

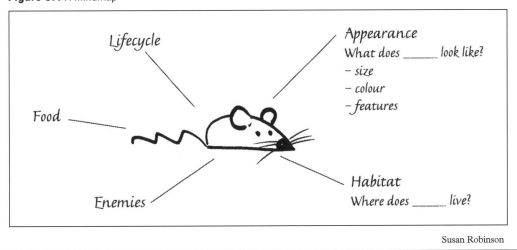

Susan Robinson

Handout 2

Finding Resources

Before you can find resources you must develop a list of useful search words for use when you search the book catalogue, CD-ROM indexes, or the Internet.

How will I know the right search terms to use?

- Look at your topic.
- Pick out the main words that describe your topic.
- Now think about *other ways of saying or spelling* any of your words.

For an assignment on Egyptian clothing and makeup try:

- 'costume' or 'fashion' instead of 'clothing';
- 'cosmetics' instead of 'make-up';
- 'jewelry' (American spelling) instead of 'jewellery' (British spelling).

Now think of *broader terms* that might describe your topic or *narrower terms* that might describe your topic.

For example, if an assignment required students to research what 'Life in Space' is like, the following terms could be generated:

Figure 8.2 Generating keywords

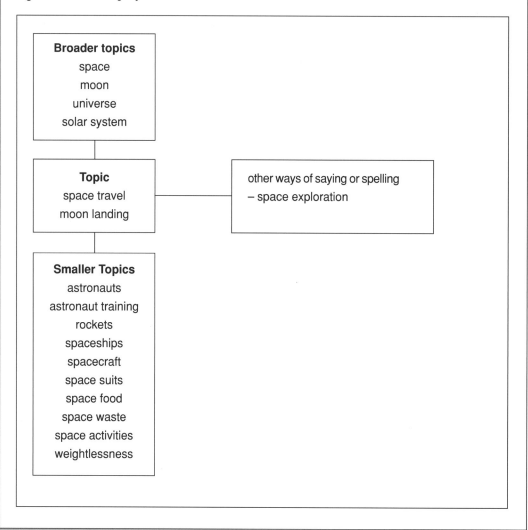

Reproduced from work by Sue Healey

Handout 3

Searching Hints
The Internet

Start with a search engine

Search engines are similar to the catalogue that you find in the library. You enter your search terms and then you are given a list of websites where you can find information.

Search engines can find a very large number of such websites. They might find more than 100 000 websites for you to look at!

How could it find so many? Imagine if our library catalogue not only contained the title and subject headings for each book but also contained the location of every word on a page in every book in the library. If you multiply the number of pages (say 250) by the number of books (say 40 000) that would mean that the catalogue would contain 10 million entries (260 pages x 40 000 books). That's how a search engine comes up with so many possibilities!

One search engine, AltaVista, is a good place to start. Its address is:

<www.AltaVista.digital.com>

Type this address in the window at the top of the screen where it says 'Go to' or 'Location'. The Altavista search engine will come up on your computer.

You are now ready to begin searching the worldwide web (www).

Five hints for better searching

1. Put a plus sign (+) in front of word that *must* be in documents found by the search. Do not put a space between the + and the word. For example, +geese+migration *or* +migration+salmon+river
2. Put a minus sign (-) in front of words that *should not* appear in any documents. Do not put a space between the − and the word.
3. Use double quotation marks (" ") around words that must appear next to each other. For example: "geese migration" *or* +migration+salmon+river+"spawning grounds"
4. Capitalise proper nouns – that is, names of people or places. Use lower case for all other searches.
5. Use an asterisk (*) to replace letters in words to select a range of endings. For example:+"bird*migration"+geese *or* +migration+salmon+river+"spawning ground"

Reproduced from work by Sue Healey

Internet pitfalls

The Internet can be a terrific source of up-to-date information about a huge variety of subjects – but it can also be a minefield for students with LLD. The handout on the Internet (Handout 3, above) is a useful tool but some LLD students might require more detailed instruction. Several things should be kept in mind.

Generating search items

Generating search terms can prove to be too difficult for LLD students. The flowchart shown in Figure 8.3 might be helpful for them.

Students can pick out keywords and follow these through. One word is enough to begin with. Then they can get other suitable search terms. Recognition of related words is more important than generating words because many search sites have the information on the screen. It is useful for LLD students to develop recognition of synonyms as this can make search tasks much easier. It should be remembered that extra support will be necessary for LLD students. Even if extra search words are in front of them, they might still have difficulties and need further explanation of those words.

Figure 8.3 Flowchart for generating Internet search terms

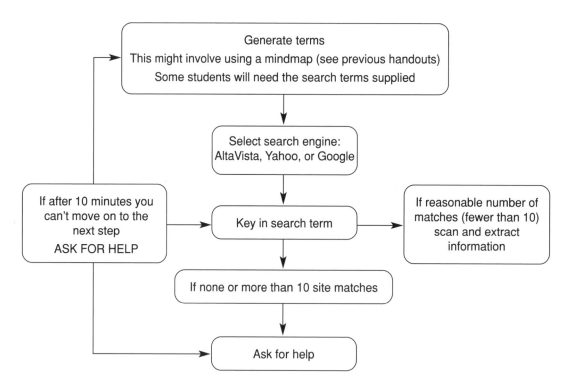

Mandy Brent, Florence Gough, Susan Robinson

Bias of Internet sites

Beware of the 'agenda' of Internet sites. These biases might not be immediately obvious to students, and it can be difficult for them to question the information that they believe must be true – because 'I found it on the Internet'.

Discernment

Effective use of the Internet requires that students be discerning about the quantity and quality of the information that they download. This is frequently beyond LLD students – who will download everything and then be overwhelmed by the amount of information they have. This can result in their giving up altogether.

LLD is often characterised by impulsivity and resistance to change. In researching on the Internet, LLD students need to be closely monitored to ensure that they are downloading appropriate material.

Brodie had an assignment that required her to research 'the Temple' (Herod's Temple).

After spending several periods in the library on the Internet searching for information, she came back with articles on the Temple Institute and the Temple Museum. She had not realised that these were not relevant to her topic. She had merely accepted all information found by the search word 'temple'.

Brodie had not been completely sure of her topic to begin with and she was therefore unsure what she was looking for. She was thus not equipped to check that her search was relevant to her topic.

Teacher involvement

Teachers need to provide some students with site addresses. This is necessary to reduce the amount of time and energy wasted on fruitless searching. Teachers should visit websites frequently to ensure that information is still available at that address, that the information is accessible, and that the site is updated regularly.

It is best not to start on a wide search of the Internet but set tasks where students go to structured sites.

Follow up on efforts to search for information – to point out errors and frustrations. To find out where problems are, teachers and resource staff need to try the search themselves before students start their research.

Alternatives to the Internet

Remember that books and CD-ROMs are still excellent sources of information. The Internet might not have the best and most easily sourced information.

Books might be better because the teacher or librarian is able to choose the level of difficulty of the text (for example, from a basic pictorial book to a more complex publication). The layouts of some books are often easier to follow than the Internet, thus helping the reader through the text. Hardcopy is often easier to read, and being able to flick between pages is useful for many students. Reading information on a computer screen can be difficult for those students who are already experiencing problems with reading and understanding the printed word.

Just as LLD students can download too much information from the Internet, poor readers often photocopy reams of information from books. This can be very unproductive work and a poor use of time. To limit this we suggest that teachers set a size limit before students start and decide how much information will be needed. For example, if the project is to be three pages, students might need only an A4-sheet size of information.

Many LLD students have difficulty generating vocabulary and
s can cause difficulties in getting started on the research process.
prevent their feeling overwhelmed by the task, it is important to
ld up skills slowly. There are additional steps that can be added
re students confront text.

PLANNING
REASONING
REFLECTING

CHAPTER 9

Skills across the Curriculum

A variety of skills – such as notetaking, summarising, breaking work down into manageable steps, and question formation – are vital to students' success at secondary school. Some students need relatively little assistance in these skill areas but LLD students need a lot of practice in using and developing these skills across all subject areas. A broader approach to teaching these skills in a variety of subjects, not just English, is needed by many students (including LLD students). Such an approach can significantly improve students' comprehension and prepare them for more complex tasks.

Notetaking

Students need to be taught how to take notes and must have plenty of opportunities for practice. They must:

- know why they are taking notes (that is, be aware of the purpose of the task);
- understand the vocabulary and concepts of the passage;
- be able to generate questions about the task (for example, for a chapter summary of a novel, students must ask: 'What are the main events? Who are the main characters?');
- be able to find the keywords and the main idea in a sentence or paragraph that they are to summarise; and
- make the notes relevant to the question they are answering.

Notetaking from objects or pictures

Many LLD students have difficulty generating vocabulary and this can cause difficulties in getting started on the research process. To prevent their feeling overwhelmed by the task, it is important to build up skills slowly. There are additional steps that can be added before students confront text.

Begin with visuals

Start with objects and picture-based activities (no text) when beginning a new topic. Learn to make hypotheses. Raise hypotheses from these visual materials.

Encourage questions

Encourage students to ask questions about the visuals. *Question development is a critical skill.* LLD students have particular difficulty generating questions. They will need to be taught explicitly how to form questions. (More information on this is available in the section on checksheets. Question charts can provide a useful prompt. The question chart on the 'Standard of Ur' is an example of such a chart. It can be adapted for use with text-based information. Questioning also helps introduce new vocabulary. It is important to remember that this questioning skill might not be generalised to other topics.

Notes and keywords

Take notes and generate keywords from the pictures. This helps students to begin the exploration of different ways of gathering information. They can take a guess and, if they are not sure, put a question mark after it. Adding in this step increases the verbal and written output of students.

Example 1

The Standard of Ur

The following example requires that students observe two pictures of the Standard of Ur and take notes from the picture.

The first sheet (Figure 9.1 and Table 9.1) helps the students by generating appropriate questions for them.

The second sheet (Figure 9.2 and Table 9.2) is more difficult, requiring that students generate similar sorts of questions for themselves.

Breaking down information into clear boxes and working on small topics at a time helps students to organise their notes properly so that, when it comes to producing some writing, they are in the best possible position to write a sentence or paragraph about each topic.

Figure 9.1 The Standard of Ur – Peace Side

© Copyright The British Museum

This task can be given to the class as a whole and used as a model for further research. It is probable that LLD students will need help generating the questions if they are to generate reasonable notes. It may even be necessary to provide them with the questions.

Once taught, LLD students might find the grid useful for many types of research – but they might need to be reminded. It is probable that they will not generalise this activity to other topics.

Table 9.1 Standard of Ur Handout 1

Clothes	Food
Is everyone dressed the same? What differences can you see?	What do you think might be contained in the packs for the king? From the other things the people are carrying can you tell what sources of food the people of Sumer had?
Animals	**Types of work carried out**
What animals can you identify? How are they being used?	Describe what the men are doing. Is there any evidence to tell you how society was organised? Do there appear to be slaves or prisoners? What are the ordinary folk doing?
Entertainment	**Technologies**
Can you see any musical instruments?	From this panel of the box can you work out some of the technologies that the people of Sumer had?

Figure 9.2 The Standard of Ur – War Side

Table 9.2 Standard of Ur Handout 2

Weapons	Use of animals during war
Armour	Treatment of prisoners
Fighting methods	Any other interesting facts

Starting at the visual level leads easily into follow-up work that can be adapted to different levels of ability. In the ideal situation, the following process will occur.

- Students are encouraged to work in pairs (using different coloured pens) and swap pictures to see what others can find from the picture. This activity leads well into a notetaking exercise as pictures generate keywords and 'bites of information'.

- The task can be extended to a notetaking exercise. As students build up a list of words and ideas from the picture they can then write a paragraph. They can start their paragraph with a simple topic sentence and then expand in the rest of the paragraph from the information in front of them.

- Students can exchange their paragraphs and work on refining the notes taken.

Notetaking is difficult for LLD students and adding the visual level breaks the task down further.

Example 2

First year history research assignment

The following history assignment on Tutankhamen's tomb requires that students take notes to answer a number of questions (Handout 1). A notetaking sheet is supplied to ensure that students have enough material to answer each of the questions adequately (Handout 2).

Tutankhamen's Tomb Handout 1

Tutankhamen's Tomb: Research Assignment

Instructions

In 1922 the British archaeologist Howard Carter discovered the tomb of Pharaoh Tutankhamen. When he entered the tomb he uncovered an amazing collection of artefacts that revealed many aspects about life in ancient Egypt.

Your assignment is to imagine it is 1930 and that you have been asked to produce a guide to the tomb and some of its important contents. This guide could take two main forms:

- an archaeological report written by Howard Carter; or
- a guide written for tourists visiting the site.

Whichever of these you choose to do, your guide must include the following sections:

- a brief background on Howard Carter (for example, previous discoveries, events leading up to the tomb opening);
- a general description of the Valley of the Kings where the site is located;
- a description of the opening of the first room (called the antechamber) and a general description of its appearance; this description should involve selecting two objects from the antechamber and providing a more detailed description of these objects (for example, the throne or animal couches);
- a description of the second room (called the burial chamber), including details on the wooden shrine, the stone sarcophagus, and the coffins;
- a description of two objects found in the third room (called the treasury); these could be the model boats or the golden shrine;
- an explanation of why this was such an important discovery; and
- a brief mention of the 'curse of the pharaohs'.

Reproduced from work done by Tintern AGGS History Department

Tutankhamen's Tomb Handout 2

Tutankhamen's Tomb: Research Assignment

Notetaking Sheet

1. Describe Howard Carter's background. What were the discoveries he had made before the Tomb of Tutankhamen and what led up to the opening of the tomb?
   [Note that a CD-ROM worksheet is supplied.]

2. Describe the Valley of the Kings where the tomb is.
   [Note that a photo is supplied in a textbook.]

Reproduced from work done by Tintern AGGS History Department

In Handout 2, this layout is supplied for all questions. If students have particular difficulty with notetaking, extra questions could be supplied within the grid.

Taking notes from written material

Notetaking from written material can be helped with the following advice to students.

- Read all of the passage before you start to take notes.
- It is often best to read aloud. This helps you to understand.
- You might understand better if someone reads the information to you.
- Re-read the information paragraph by paragraph.
- At the end of each paragraph ask yourself: 'Do I understand this?'.
- Write down the main points in short, simple phrases. You do not need to write full sentences.
- Spread your work out so that you have room to add information and so that you can read your notes clearly.
- You can draw attention to main points in several ways. Use a highlighter. Use different colours for main points and details or for different topics. Make pencil notes in the margin. Asterisk important points.
- You can organise your information in several different ways including tables, flowcharts, grids (such as the note-taking sheet for the 'Standard of Ur'), webs, graphic organisers (such as a 'mindmap').

Example

Painting assignment

The following example illustrates taking notes from written material (as well as study of artistic technique).

Figure 9.3 Painting Assignment

Painting Assignment

Portraiture:

Paintings, like other art forms, are concerned with ideas, not merely with an imitation of appearance for its own sake. Paintings are abstractions of objects, ideas, and events. Only a tree can be a tree; a painting of a tree is not a tree but a painting: an interpretation and abstraction of a tree through the use of pigment.

Look at Rembrandt and his use of colour and technique to render likenesses. Look at his treatment of his subject. That is, does he view his subject with kindness or harshly? Compare and contrast Rembrandt with a modern portrait painter – William Dobell. Is Dobell's work a 'true likeness' and how does it compare with Rembrandt's?

You will need to research into their backgrounds to find out how they were influenced by their cultures and attitudes of the time.

Hints on how to approach this assignment.

1. Research their backgrounds – that is, date of birth, country, cultural background (that is, poor/rich) and influences.
2. Select two works of each artist – study the works and then compare them. Look at their differences, look at their similarities. Look at the techniques of the artists and the colours used.
3. What was the purpose of the work? Did they differ?
4. Finally, do you like the works – why? Which work do you prefer and why?

GOOD LUCK!   ENJOY!

From Brent, Gough and Robinson 1988

Figure 9.4 Painting assignment; table to be completed

	Rembrandt	**Dobell**
Born		
Country		
Family background		
Factors affecting development		
	Rembrandt painting (name)	**Modern artist's painting (name)**
Technique		
Colour		
Purpose of the work		
Similarities		
Differences		

From Brent, Gough and Robinson 1988

Taking notes from spoken information (including TV and video)

LLD students can find the taking of notes from oral material extremely difficult. The process involves simultaneously watching and listening to information, comprehending it, and then having to summarise it. As well as deciding what to write, students must also perform the difficult physical task of writing – while the information continues to come at them.

There are, however, some strategies that students can employ to give themselves the best chance of taking down the necessary information. Teachers can provide the following hints.

- Be prepared with pen and paper.
- Make sure that you know why you are taking notes.
- Have the questions that you have to answer written in front of you, and make sure that the questions are clearly in your mind.

- Listen carefully.
- Listen for the important ideas and keywords and write them down.
- Be aware that teachers often give cues about important points by using words such as: 'first', 'second', 'one important point . . .'.
- When you are making notes write only a few words about each point. You do not need to write full sentences, but you need to write enough to remember all about your point.
- In taking notes, miss out little words such as 'a', 'the', 'is', and so on.
- Learn some abbreviations for words. These might include: 'e.g.' (for example); 'etc.' (et cetera); 'tch' (teacher); 'sch' (school).
- Leave a space between points so that you can add information later.
- Read your notes through as soon as you can (to be sure that you can understand them). This is a good time to add any extra details that you can remember.

For those students who simply cannot master the techniques of taking notes, teachers might need to:

- use notetaking sheets with keywords and pictographs and/or cloze activities (in which students have to place the keyword in the passage);
- give key information on tape, so that students can listen to it several times, and so that the tape can be stopped or rewound if necessary to allow students to write down key information;
- allow LLD students to obtain help by using the notes of other students;
- check the comprehension of the material by LLD students and check the use of any abbreviations.

Video proforma

To ensure that students are taking adequate notes from film texts it is advisable to prepare students well, before they watch the film. We have developed a proforma that can be adapted to all film texts. The proforma can be adapted to a cloze activity completed after students finish watching the film. The proforma consists of the following parts.

1. Simple summary of events

This summary should be very brief – only a short paragraph that gives students an idea of what the plot is about. LLD students have problems absorbing large amounts of information, and a summary that is too long might only confuse them. The summary can also outline some of the main themes in the film.

2. Characters

A list of the main characters should be supplied with a short description of the character in the form of a word list. Introduce new vocabulary by linking new complicated words to simpler words that students already know.

3. Vocabulary

Students are encouraged to look for words that can create confusion – especially if they have multiple meanings.

> A fourth year student watched *The Mission* in which reference is made to a 'religious order'. She thought that the word 'order' referred to food orders, and was very confused by its repeated use in another sense in the film.

4. Background information

It might be necessary to provide a brief context to the film, especially if the subject matter of the film is significantly removed from the students' own experiences. Providing such a context might take the form of a short explanation of the political, historical, or social conventions portrayed in the film. It is important to find out what the students do know, because there can be significant gaps in this area.

> One LLD student watched the film *Titanic*. Because the setting of the film seemed to her to be a long time ago, she assumed that this meant that the *Titanic* itself was a very old ship. She was therefore not at all surprised that it sank 'because it was old'. She had completely missed the significance of the ship's sinking.

These kinds of misunderstandings are common. In a preteaching class, students can verbally brainstorm all the things they know about the film, and misunderstandings such as these can be corrected.

5. Film sequence, including film elements

Important scenes in the film should be isolated. Questions about each scene should be provided for students before they watch the film so that they can be alert and focused for the information. Scenes vary in their individual focus. For example, teachers can point out that a given scene might emphasise an important sequence of events, or character development, or music, or lighting, or sound, or close-up shots, or long shots, and so on. The students need assistance in directing their attention to these various elements so they better appreciate what is important in a given scene.

6. Check for comprehension by compare and contrast

After watching the film, a good way to check for comprehension, to develop themes and to prepare students for writing, is to *compare and contrast* characters, music and scenes in the film.

Example of using video proforma

The following is an abbreviated example of the use of a video proforma using the film *One Flew Over the Cuckoo's Nest*.

One Flew Over the Cuckoo's Nest

Video Proforma

1. Simple summary of events

One Flew Over the Cuckoo's Nest is set in a mental hospital and the patients have set routines to follow each day. Most of the patients have chosen to be in the mental hospital (and they are therefore called 'voluntary patients'). McMurphy is in prison but he wants to come to the mental hospital because he wants to avoid prison work. He pretends to be mad and he is sent to the mental hospital. At the mental hospital he tries to change the routines. Nurse Ratched does not like McMurphy and does not like the changes that he tries to make.

2. Characters

Randle P. McMurphy is violent, resentful, angry, lazy, belligerent, and aggressive.

Nurse Ratched is controlling and expressionless.

3. Vocabulary

Some words that have much the same meaning in the film are:

mental illness; looney; nut; mental defective

institution; hospital

4. Background information

One Flew Over the Cuckoo's Nest is very critical of aspects of society in 1975 – especially how people were labelled according to race, mental health, and sex.

The film is about power in society and asks questions about:

- the treatment of people in mental hospitals;
- racial prejudice against Afro-Americans (Negroes);
- the destruction of Native American (Indian) race and culture;
- psychiatric treatment (therapy);
- the role of women.

5. Film sequence and film elements

1. The film opens with mountains and wide-open spaces. What is the background music?
2. There is a scene featuring a 'therapy circle',
   - Who is controlling the conversation in the circle? Who has the power?
   - What are the women doing? How would you describe the women?
   - What are the men doing? How would you describe the men?

6. Checking for comprehension

Contrast two characters. For example, contrast Nurse Ratched and McMurphy.

Nurse Ratched	McMurphy
conservative (likes things to be the same and doesn't like change)	radical (wants to change the way things are done)
order and regulations	freedom

Note the words in brackets in the box above. Explanatory words attached to complex words or phrases help with understanding.

Students can be asked to give examples of these characteristics from the film. This sort of compare/contrast brainstorm leads well into themes.

Checksheets – setting a framework

Checksheets set frameworks about how to approach a particular problem or activity. Checksheets contain a list of steps that students must follow to complete a task. The tasks can be broad-ranging. For example, the task might be completing an assignment, or perhaps working out how to use public transport. The task is broken down into easily workable segments.

For example, to look up and ring a number in the telephone book, a checksheet might look like that shown in Table 9.3.

Table 9.3 Checksheet for approaching a task

Question	Answer
What do I have to do first?	Find the telephone book.
What do I have to look up?	Coopers Computer Store
What do I have to next?	1. Turn to 'C' in the phone book.
	2. Using what I know about the alphabet, locate Coopers Computer Store.
	3. Write down the telephone number.
	4. Ring Coopers and ask my question.

Students often have knowledge but have difficulty working through the steps needed to complete tasks in the way that is required. To be independent they need to have some way of knowing *how* to approach tasks. Assignments can cause great difficulty because they are complex and there is a sequence of many steps involved in their completion. Students might forget what they have to do or what they have already done. Keeping on task can be a problem for many students. Checksheets are designed to provide the necessary framework to keep students on a task right through to its completion.

Daniel's geography assignment required him to plan a trip around Britain. He began to plan his route with assistance from a support person. Later, he forgot what he had already done. He started again, with another helper. Later, he had to start again with another helper. This helper discovered Daniel's other plans and developed a simple checksheet to help him with his organisation. The helper also developed a grid for place, distance travelled, mode of transport and features attached to a map of Britain.

Table 9.4 Checksheet for approaching an assignment

Question	Answer
What am I being asked to do?	[Student fills in answer; for example, plan a trip around Britain.]
Where am I going to start my trip?	[Student fills in answer; for example, London.]
Where am I going to go first?	[Student fills in answer; for example, York.]
Set up information grid, and enter information on information grid.	[See Table 9.5]
How far is it?	[Student fills in answer.]
How will I find out how far it is?	[Student fills in answer; for example, use an atlas.]
How am I going to get there?	[Student fills in answer.]
What will I see when I get there?	[Student fills in answer.]
How will I find out what to see?	[Student fills in answer; for example, tourist guides.]
Where am I going to go next?	[Student fills in answer.]

Table 9.5 Information grid for an assignment

Places	Distance	Mode of transport
London to York	196 miles	aeroplane
York to Glasgow	211 miles	car

Students will need help to work through all the steps required and to work out the questions they have to ask themselves. Initially the students will need to be given the questions and it might be necessary to supply them every time the students begin a new task. In time, students might be able to generate their own questions (although this will not necessarily occur).

Frameworks in the form of checksheets can give point-by-point instruction – a sort of 'recipe' for how to work through the task. Eventually, the use of checksheets helps students to 'internalise' the process of going about the task. They learn to ask themselves the appropriate questions. When students develop the skill of thinking about how to approach a task they are using *metacognitive strategies*. These enhance effective learning. The use of questions helps to structure thinking – to work out sequence and determine the information that is needed. These questions can form the checksheet.

For example, an assignment on infectious disease investigation might take the form shown in the handout.

Infectious disease handout

Infectious Diseases Assignment

Instructions

This assignment requires you to research an infectious disease, and to present your findings in a written report of 300–400 words and a 4–5 minute talk to the class. You are expected to use at least three sources and reference them correctly in a bibliography.

Checklist	
Question/steps	**Answer**
What am I being asked to do?	Write a report and give a talk on a disease.
What do I have to do first?	Choose a disease (for example, tinea).
What do I need to find out about?	Ask questions about how the disease can be caught.
What are the symptoms? What does the word 'symptom' mean?	[Student fills in answer.]
How is it prevented or cured? What does the word 'prevention' mean?	[Student fills in answer.]
What are the questions? What causes tinea?	[Student fills in answer.]
What would I search for in databases, Internet, or books?	[Student fills in answer; for example, tinea.]
Take notes from information.	I have to use three sources, so use a grid or cards.

Checksheets can be made into flowcharts, grids or cycles to help students to break down the task into small logical steps.

Students are required to research a huge variety of subjects at every level of secondary school. LLD students might never be able to perform this research independently. The strategies outlined in this chapter do require support from general classroom teachers and aim to encourage good research and notetaking habits. This will aid students in the next step of the process – writing.

LLD students have difficulty generating vocabulary and
...n cause difficulties in getting started on the research process.
...vent their feeling overwhelmed by the task it is important to
...p skills slowly. There are additional steps that can be added
...students confront text.

PLANNING
REASONING
REFLECTING

CHAPTER 10

Writing

Introduction

Teaching students with language disabilities to write essays, reports, letters and narratives is a demanding and time-consuming task that requires cooperation across year levels, a high level of interaction with students and many opportunities for student practice. Not all students will become independent writers but the process of learning to write their thoughts as clearly as possible has enormous benefits for their cognitive and language development.

Generally, written language is more explicit than spoken language. Words must be carefully chosen so that the communication is clear and concise. As they progress with writing, students need to use more complex grammar than they would when speaking. They need to monitor their work, asking themselves questions such as:

- Am I answering the question?
- Is that the most appropriate word?
- Does that sentence make sense?

They need to check that their ideas are logically sequenced and that they are achieving their goal of communication with the reader.

It is through the writing process that underlying language difficulties become more apparent. These include deficits in vocabulary, comprehension, planning, sequencing words, sentence construction, expressing ideas in paragraphs, identifying themes, summarising, brainstorming and developing topics. Students and teachers alike can identify starting points, along with the level of questioning that students need to edit and reflect.

Adolescent language

During adolescence, comprehension, oral language and written language continue to be developed and refined. Typically this is shown in a greater understanding and use of:

- subordinate clauses (which enable students to write more complex sentences);
- adjectives and adverbs (which tell more about emotions);

- more elaborate phrases (for example: the tall, gnarled, old woman);

- an expanded topic-specific vocabulary;

- greater social understanding and knowledge of world events along with the ability to place these events within the context of their class discussions and written work;

- increased social and world knowledge when reading texts (thus increasing their comprehension of these texts); and

- cognitive flexibility to see multiple meanings in individual words and texts.

If students cannot explain their ideas logically aloud, they are likely to have similar problems in written work. LLD students might not have fully developed comprehension and spoken language in relation to their peers, and writing is consequently difficult for them. It requires the synthesis of many skills that LLD students find difficult.

The following examples from students illustrate typical difficulties in the areas of content, organisation, grammar and spelling.

Example 1: Meg, aged 13 years

> She opened the lasted boks and the door creak open, Aligandra herde footsteps quilte turned and teas folling. It was mum she looked cross she quickly moved her hand and pointed out of the room. I ran out. I run down the stars jumt on my bike I saw my friend

This piece of writing has a number of problems, including:

- poor sequence;

- major points poorly linked;

- changing personal pronouns from third person ('she') to first person ('I');

- limited use of conjunctions;

- overuse of 'and';

- fragments of sentences;

- poor use of punctuation;

- phonetic and non-phonetic spelling errors;

- the story continues for several pages but fails to reach a conclusion; and

- vocabulary is limited and repetitive.

Example 2: Mike, aged 13 years

> They are franly kint of Bird in the world and the cutest. they need to be feed daly and water if you want eggs to eart. They have fheavers and wings and go bok bok or cheap cheep.

Problems in this piece of writing include:

- limited in both quantity and quality;
- limited background knowledge about chickens (unable to describe their characteristics and habits);
- irregular and inappropriate use of capitals and punctuation; and
- spelling is so irregular that it is very difficult to read (for example, 'franly' for 'friendly'; 'fheavers' for 'feathers'; 'eart' for 'eat').

Mike's spelling difficulties are so great that it is probable that he will not be able to use a spell-checker independently.

Example 3: Steven, aged 17 years

In response to the question 'What might be Shakespeare's reason for creating a situation in which Macbeth sees a seemingly supernatural dagger?', a fifth year student wrote:

> Shakespear could have created this situation where he sees the supernatural daggers all in his mind because the witches have placed this immage in and want him to get scared. I believe that Shakespears main reason is for Macbeth to get scared and not follow through with the murder.

Problems in this writing include:

- pronoun confusion (unclear whether Steven is referring to Shakespeare or to Macbeth);
- the explanation shows some comprehension difficulties;
- use of 'I', not appropriate in formal writing;
- spelling difficulties; and
- sentence structure and expression are poor.

Explaining writing to LLD students

LLD students often do not understand that writing is more than good spelling and grammar. They need to be told that the purpose of most writing at school is to show understanding and explain ideas in a logical, structured way. The implied purpose of the writing task needs to be stated overtly. Students might need to ask specific overt questions such as:

- Who am I writing for?
- Why am I writing this?
- What do I already know about this topic?

The organisation skills of LLD students are helped if teachers give them a task and assessment checklist for each piece of writing. This makes explicit the steps in the process and explains how their work will be assessed.

The following example (Figure 10.1 and Figure 10.2) is from a first year assignment and indicates clearly what the students need to do and when. It is quite explicit about the steps required and the way they must be ordered to complete the assignment successfully. Support for students who have difficulty generating questions is provided by a classroom activity in Step 3 (Figure 10.2).

Figure 10.1 First year oral history project

First Year oral history project

What is an oral history project?

We are researching the lives of people who were alive during World War II, 1939–1945. These people might not have been to war, but their lives might have been affected or they might have known someone who did go to the war. Your task is to interview the person to find out more about this time in history.

This sheet will tell you step-by-step what to do. Follow each step carefully and use the 'tick box' to tick off each step once you have completed it. If you have any difficulties, ask your English teacher.

Write all of the due dates into your record book so that you know how to space your work.

STEP 1: Completed ☐

Go home and talk to your parents about this project. Think of a person you would like to interview who is over the age of 60. Try to choose a person whom you can visit easily. You could interview a grandparent, a neighbour, an elderly relative, or friend.

STEP 2: Completed ☐

Ring or visit the person and ask for permission to interview him or her. Remember to tell the person that you are going to tape the interview.

STEP 3: Completed ☐

In class, make up a list of interview questions. Your teacher will give you some ideas. Make sure you show your teacher the final copy of your interview questions.

Your final copy of interview questions is due on 10/11 June.

STEP 4: Completed ☐

Make an interview time with your person between 10 June and 19 July and complete the interview.

STEP 5: Completed ☐

Take these things to the interview: paper, pens, interview questions, tape recorder, blank tape.

Complete your interview. Remember to tape it. (Don't forget to do a sound check to make sure that you can hear the person speaking on tape.)

Write down any follow-up questions on paper.

STEP 6: Completed ☐

On Tuesday 20 July, bring your tape with the interview on it to school. Your teacher will show you how to take point-form notes from the interview tape.

STEP 7: Completed ☐

Take notes from the interview tape. If there is one important sentence, you could use it as a quote, but don't forget 'inverted commas'.

Notes from the interview must be finished by Tuesday 27 July.

STEP 8: Completed ☐

Group your notes under headings. For example: home life
food
clothing

You could use a highlighter pen to do this step.

Discard any points that you think are not important.

Karyn Murray

Figure 10.2 Presenting your oral history project

Presenting your oral history project

During the next two weeks, you will be working on the presentation of your oral history assignment. Before you begin, you must decide the following.

Will my project be a diary, letters, a scrapbook, a project book, a children's story book, a series of postcards, a travel journal? Do you have any other ideas?

Will I write in the present tense (I am going to war) or past tense (I went to war in 1939)?

Will it be written in the first person (I pretend to be a person in the story) or the third person (I tell the story)?

What pictures, photographs, newspaper cuttings, drawings, or memorabilia will I use to illustrate the story?

Once you have decided these things, begin your project. Remember to write a draft of the written material and check it carefully for spelling mistakes, and punctuation and grammatical errors.

Don't forget to make your work neat and tidy, and to make the whole project attractively presented.

Your project is due on 17 August.

Karyn Murray

Comprehension – filling in the gaps for LLD students

Due to poor comprehension, LLD students have gaps in their knowledge that should not be underestimated. Failure to spend time on this has a direct effect on the quantity and quality of written work. Significant gaps in students' schemata (the experiences and knowledge of a topic and related topics that students have stored in their memories) mean that LLD students typically do not make connections with other relevant information.

LLD students might not be able to 'read between the lines' and might not appreciate complex psychological insights and characterisations. This limits their understanding of what they read. As a result, their writing lacks depth.

If students do not understand the topic it is very difficult to write much or to write clearly. Poor comprehension also impacts significantly on the writing tasks of planning, revising and evaluating. A good way to check comprehension is through the notetaking and brainstorming tasks outlined below. When working with students with LLD, always check what they already know about the topic and what they need to find out.

Example 1

> An English project required students to plan a dinner party and invite guests who were no longer living. Among other things, students had to design a menu, send out invitations and write a conversation between the three guests. The LLD student could not think of anyone. He had heard of Princess Diana and knew that she was a lady who had died. He did not know who her husband was or who was in the royal family. He also could not think of any American food to feed his American guest, Elvis Presley, despite having eaten lots of hamburgers and hot dogs, and despite having spent hours watching American movies and 'sitcoms'.

Example 2

> The class was asked to describe the character of Fingerbone Bill from the novel *Storm Boy* by Colin Thiele.
> An LLD student described Fingerbone as the 14-year-old Aboriginal friend of Storm Boy even though the text described him as ' … a wiry, wizened man with a flash of white teeth and a jolly black face as screwed-up and wrinkled as an old boot'.
> The student was amazed to discover that the character was an adult. She had also not connected his knowledge of animals and the land to his Aboriginal culture.

These examples clearly illustrates that general classroom methods of introducing a writing task might not be sufficient for many LLD adolescents. Considerable time and effort is needed to extract what students know and then to determine what needs to be researched. Preteaching is required to make connections to prior knowledge and to fill in the gaps, along with brainstorming, planning, and starter sentences.

Vocabulary – the elusive words

Vocabulary is highly correlated with general language ability and is considered to be a predictor of academic success and competence in reading and writing. On any measure of vocabulary, LLD students perform poorly. In both spoken and written language, they generally do not use a variety of words and the words that they do use are rarely longer than seven letters. This is an external manifestation of the difficulty that is at the root of their language disorder. They find it difficult to process the rapidly changing sounds that make up each individual word and the strings of words that form sentences. It follows that longer words are harder to remember.

The vocabulary of many textbook glossaries is too complex for LLD students and often needs to be simplified. Teaching the vocabulary of a new topic within the normal classroom might not be enough for many LLD students. They need time to reinforce new words before and after a topic is presented in class. In particular, attention needs to be given to the following aspects of teaching vocabulary.

- Students need to *hear* new words and require help with pronunciation.

- New words need to be divided into syllables and phonograms and base words need to be identified. For example, students might know 'character' but not 'characterisation'. Dividing words into syllables to help memory and spelling is difficult for many students to do independently. With some related words, the pronunciation changes markedly because of extra syllables (for example, 'nation' and 'national'; 'define' and 'definition'). The words sound different and students can have trouble recognising the relationship between them. These sorts of connections must be made explicit. Time does not allow all words to be dealt with in this detailed way but it is important that keywords are.

- Take words that students know about a topic and use those as a basis for expansion.

- It might be opportune to revisit skills such as spelling. Many students can improve their spelling in adolescence. Doing so gives them confidence to write more and increases their independence with spell-checkers.

- LLD students must attach new vocabulary to words they already know or to visual images or to concept maps. For example, they need to associate a new word such as 'belligerent' with a known word such as 'angry'. This helps develop comprehension and the ability to access new vocabulary at a later stage.

The language of learning

It should never be assumed that students understand the language of learning. There are many words used across the curriculum that can be confusing to LLD students.

Students can find words difficult because they can have multiple meanings and because these multiple meanings can require quite different responses from students. For example, 'illustrate' can mean 'draw', but it can also mean 'describe in words'.

Table 10.1 contains typical examples of words from 'the language of learning' that might cause difficulties for students with LLD. The words have different meanings – often subtle – and it should not be assumed that students will appreciate these differences without explanation.

Table 10.1 'Language of learning' terminology

compare	present	reference	comprehension
contrast	illustrate	opposite	vocabulary
list	collect	characteristics	evaluate
define	calculate	plural	source
identify	approximate	omitted	issue
explain	evaluate	express	argumentative
describe	text	predict	
produce	refer	evidence	
consider	represent	context	

It is helpful to use a simple sentence rather than a synonym to explain the meaning of these words. The *Cobuild Dictionary* (1997) has simple definitions followed by sentences that show how the word can be used. For example:

Define: 'If you *define* something you show, describe, or state clearly what it is and what its limits are, or what it is like'.

Describe: 'If you *describe* a person, object, event, or situation you say what they are like or what happened'.

A student in science was asked to draw up a table. The teacher was astonished to see the boy using a ruler to measure the table at which he was sitting. When asked what he was doing he replied that he was measuring it for size so he could draw it. The student had completely misunderstood what the teacher meant by drawing a table. This inflexibility in vocabulary and failure to understand the multiple meanings of words is common in LLD students.

Brainstorming

Use of brainstorming

Generating sufficient vocabulary and ideas to write is an early and specific stage in the writing process at which many LLD students falter.

Brainstorming is an excellent strategy to help problem writers get started. During brainstorming, students say aloud all the ideas and vocabulary that they feel relate to the topic under discussion. This important oral activity precedes written work and allows the students to trigger ideas for writing. Students find out what they already know and identify if they need more information.

Brainstorming is an excellent group activity because students can 'bounce' ideas off one another. Following the brainstorming, students need to organise the ideas and information. This can be worked into a diagram or flowchart – which is then available as a basis for writing, revising, and retaining information.

LLD students need extra help in the following areas.

Generating ideas

Students might need a picture, photograph, drawing, video or personal experience before being able to generate ideas and vocabulary. Considerable time might be required in doing this because the generation of ideas and vocabulary is a fundamental problem for LLD students. With the support of pictures and diagrams, students find it easier to generate ideas to describe in words. However, interpreting feelings and emotions and generating abstract language can still be extremely difficult.

Organisation

Students might require extra help in *organising* the brainstormed word lists to make appropriate associations and to produce a suitable sequence of ideas. They might require assistance in relating their information to the original topic. This is best achieved by working out a framework of questions to answer.

Writing a report about his work experience, John brainstormed all that he could remember about the experience. This was then structured by inserting key questions such as:

- What jobs did you do?
- Who did you work with?
- What did you enjoy?
- What did you do well?
- Did you make any mistakes?
- Did you enjoy it?

By answering these questions John was able to generate enough information to write his report.

Students might have difficulty putting their ideas into a coherent order. Diagrams can be useful.

To get good results, it is important to spend time in the steps of brainstorming and organising. However, in offering this extra help, teachers should be aware of the following potential problems.

Generalising

Students might find it difficult to repeat this process on another occasion without assistance. LLD students have difficulty generalising skills and processes from one situation to another. Students need help to decide which information to discard and which information to retain and apply in other situations.

Verbalising

Students need help to verbalise the connections between the ideas. This verbalisation is important because it checks students' understanding of what has occurred.

Example of brainstorming

The following is an excellent example of a general class brainstorming exercise. It provided all the words the students needed to write and the teacher also provided an introductory paragraph for those students who needed it.

Figure 10.3 Annotated portion of 'The Jaguar'

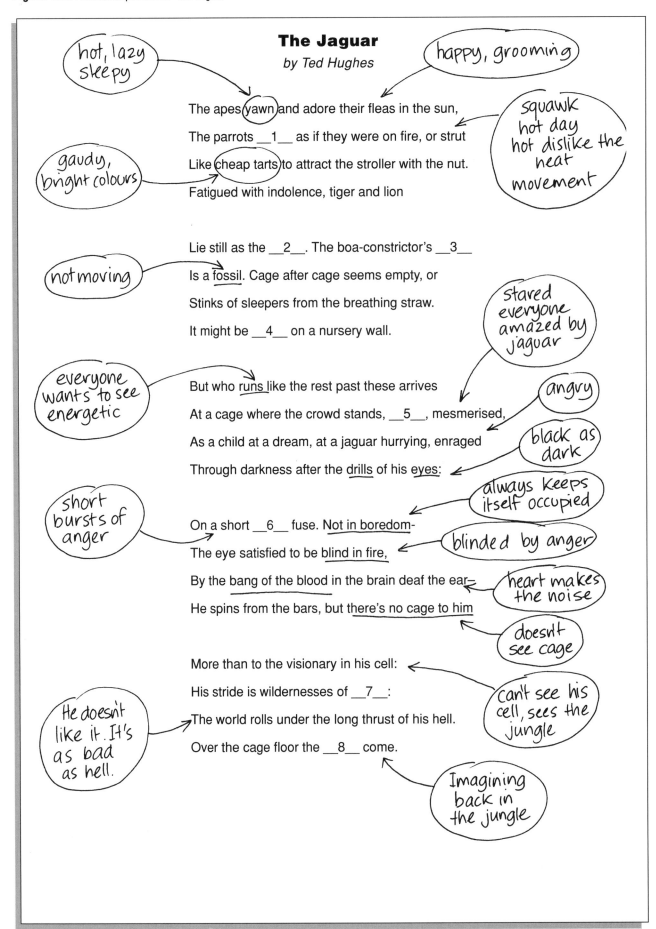

The Jaguar
by Ted Hughes

hot, lazy sleepy

happy, grooming

The apes (yawn) and adore their fleas in the sun,

squawk hot day hot dislike the heat movement

The parrots __1__ as if they were on fire, or strut

gaudy, bright colours

Like (cheap tarts) to attract the stroller with the nut.

Fatigued with indolence, tiger and lion

Lie still as the __2__. The boa-constrictor's __3__

not moving

Is a fossil. Cage after cage seems empty, or

Stinks of sleepers from the breathing straw.

It might be __4__ on a nursery wall.

stared everyone amazed by jaguar

everyone wants to see energetic

But who runs like the rest past these arrives

angry

At a cage where the crowd stands, __5__, mesmerised,

black as dark

As a child at a dream, at a jaguar hurrying, enraged

Through darkness after the drills of his eyes:

always keeps itself occupied

short bursts of anger

On a short __6__ fuse. Not in boredom-

blinded by anger

The eye satisfied to be blind in fire,

By the bang of the blood in the brain deaf the ear-

heart makes the noise

He spins from the bars, but there's no cage to him

doesn't see cage

More than to the visionary in his cell:

His stride is wildernesses of __7__:

Can't see his cell, sees the jungle

He doesn't like it. It's as bad as hell.

The world rolls under the long thrust of his hell.

Over the cage floor the __8__ come.

Imagining back in the jungle

Exercise by Chris Millgate-Smith based on poem 'The Jaguar' from *Hawk in the Rain* by Ted Hughes.
Reprinted with kind permission of Faber and Faber Ltd.

Figure 10.4 Exercise on 'The Jaguar'

The Jaguar

1 Read poem carefully, several times. With your partner, agree on a word to fit each gap. Write them in, in pencil.

2 Check your words against those in the original poem. How close were you to the meaning of the original? Which do you prefer?

3 Write in the missing words from the actual poem.

4 Circle in blue all the animals referred to in stanzas 1 and 2.

5 Circle in red all the words used to describe these animals' behaviour.

6 Underline in blue all the words and phrases which describe the jaguar's appearance.

7 Underline all the words and phrases which show how the jaguar feels.

8 Make notes around the poem to record your thoughts and feelings about any of the animals.

9 Jot down questions about anything that puzzles you.

10 Theme boxes – look at your circled and underlined words. See how many you can link together as being connected with the same theme, or idea.

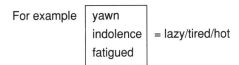

For example | yawn / indolence / fatigued | = lazy/tired/hot

11 Practise reading the poem aloud, in pairs. If you have time, try to learn it by heart.

Exercise by Chris Millgate-Smith based on poem 'The Jaguar' from *Hawk in the Rain* by Ted Hughes. Reprinted with kind permission of Faber and Faber Ltd.

Brainstorming can be used to prepare students to write specific essay genres (for example, 'compare and contrast' essays). Attach 'compare' and 'contrast' to the simpler words 'same' and 'different', respectively. One LLD student was amazed to discover that 'compare/contrast' meant that she had to say how things were the *same* and how things were *different*. The contrasting of ideas with their opposites also provides an excellent method of checking comprehension and leads into identifying themes that can be written about. The identification of themes is difficult for LLD students and can be traced back to earlier difficulties in grouping words into classes.

Getting organised – the plan and process

Additional steps for LLD students

Direct teaching of writing is beneficial for all students and gives LLD students much-needed structure and guidance. An additional step for LLD students is to model the thinking and 'inner talk' that capable writers use as part of the process of preparing to write. This helps students develop strong visualisations and allows them to generate the vocabulary they need. Many of these visualisation techniques are discussed by Nanci Bell in the programme *Visualizing and Verbalizing* (1991). Intensive teaching of this strategy might be more appropriate in individual sessions and preteaching classes.

As background to studying the book *Goodnight Mr Tom*, students needed to understand about the bombing of London during World War II. The task was broken down into steps and students were asked to describe:

- sounds heard;
- amount of destruction (size and shape);
- colours;
- numbers of people and their feelings;
- smells;
- what time of day; and
- proximity of the bombing.

Then the teacher talked about the thinking processes out loud as he organised the material ready to write.

- Where does this information belong? Yes it goes in sounds. I could use this in my first paragraph.

The thinking and organising process is then followed for other steps in the process above.

Notetaking – keywords and ideas

To teach notetaking, begin with a simple passage. Find the keywords or ideas and place them in a web structure or chart. Attach key information to these keywords. Using this information, ask students to write a short summary paragraph in their own words. This process builds up vocabulary and comprehension and provides a simple plan before the students write. Once the summary paragraph has been edited and completed, the students' work can be dictated back to them as a spelling exercise.

Julie was required to read an article from the newspaper about whales and write a paragraph about its contents (see Figure 10.5). She needed assistance to identify the keywords. Once they had been identified, she placed the keywords in a web, connected them with sentences (Figure 10.6) and answered questions until she had enough information to write a paragraph (Figure 10.7).

Figure 10.5 Newspaper article on saving whale

Herald Sun, Monday, October 19, 1998

WHALES TRUCKED TO SAFER WATERS

VOLUNTEERS used trucks to carry stricken whales on a 45-minute mercy dash to save a pod of pilot whales stranded in south-eastern Tasmania yesterday.

The trucks were used to take the whales on a 29km road trip from Blackman's Bay, about 50km east of Hobart, to where they could be released into the open sea.

The drama began on Saturday morning when 56 whales, the biggest close to 7m long and up to one tonne, beached themselves at Marion Bay, next to Blackman's Bay. Twenty-one died there.

Rescuers managed to get the rest back out to sea, where the bulk of a mother pod of about 100 was circling. Most were guided into deeper water, and dinghies were used to turn back any that tried to return.

Rangers also took a whale calf into deeper water and turned its head towards shore in the hope its distress calls would attract others. Four adults came.

"I've never seen this technique used before, but it got at least four back out," Tasmanian Parks and Wildlife Service director Max Kitchell said.

"We learn something each time with these strandings."

But instead of heading to the safety of open sea, the reunited pod on Saturday night turned towards the entrance of Blackman's Bay.

Despite efforts to head them off, about 50 became trapped in shallow water.

Rather than try to get the weakened and distressed animals back more than 2km to the bay entrance, rangers decided to truck them to Eaglehawk Neck, where they could be released into open sea.

Calves were lifted on to trailers and driven off.

Hydraulic lifts on the back of flat-bed trucks were used for the adults, which were lowered on to foam mattresses, covered with hessian and strapped down.

One truck, with two tonnes of whale on the back, bogged in the muddy sand and an excavator had to be called in to pull it free.

Volunteers rode precariously on the trucks' backs, continually sluicing the whales down with buckets of water.

Once back in the water at Eaglehawk Neck, the whales were guided towards the open sea.

Then came the news from Orford, 20km north, that more than 60 whales had beached themselves there and most had died.

"Just as we think we've got it under control, we get a kick in the guts." Mr Kitchell said.

He didn't know if the trucked whales would rejoin the mother pod.

-AAP

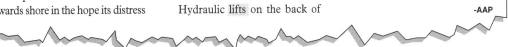

Figure 10.6 Julie's worksheet

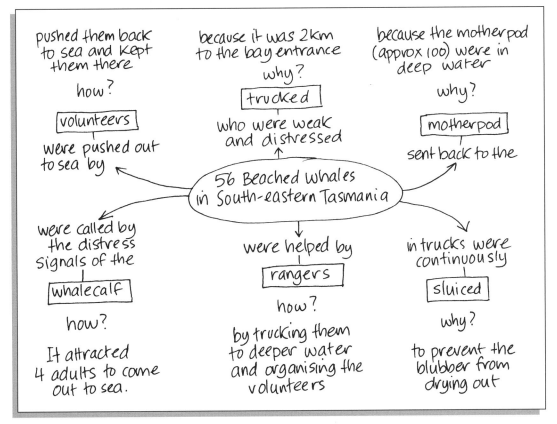

Julie (fictitious name; actual work published with permission of student)

Figure 10.7 Julie's paragraph

BEACHED WHALES

56 Whales Beached themself's in Marion Bay in Tasmania. Volunteers were there to help push them back to sea and helped to keep them in the deeper water. There was also trucks there to help the tired ones and drive them to deeper water there was a whale calf that was tatch-in back to sea and he sent out stres' signals which attracked 4 adults (whales) to come out to sea. Not all the Pod beached themself's there was 100 left back in the deep water were the volunteers were seeding them to. there was volunteers and Rangers there alt trining to help the whales as the truck's drove on the was volunteers risking there lives to sluice all the whales down.

Julie (fictitious name; work published with permission of student)

One more final edit on the computer resulted in accurate copy.

Writing checksheets

These might include brainstormed words for a topic, lists of introductory sentences, connecting words, and structure questions. See Figure 10.8.

Figure 10.8 Writing checksheets
Susan Robinson

When you are writing:
plan first;
use key words.
What are key words?

↓

Write in sentences.
What is a sentence?
What does it have at the beginning?
What does it have at the end?
How many ideas does a sentence have?

↓

Use a paragraph for each different topic.
What is a topic?

↓

Then read through what you have written.
Note any spelling mistakes and find out
how to spell the word.
Does it make sense?
Have you forgotten any little words?

↓

Re-read aloud

↓

When you edit you must read through
at least twice.

The 'keywords' approach is an effective strategy used to teach LLD students. Two programmes, among others, that have developed a range of strategies to teach writing in regular classrooms, and with LLD students, include:

- POWER (plan, organise, write, edit, rewrite/revise) by Englert (1992); and
- COPS (capitalisation, organisation, punctuation, spelling) by Schumaker *et al.* (1995).

Teachers might find the following checklist helpful when identifying the areas in which students are experiencing difficulty. It can also be used to identify areas that need intensive teacher-directed instruction.

Checklist for writing difficulties

1. Word retrieval, vocabulary, and sequencing
- Poor memory for subject-specific vocabulary and literate language needed for writing (as opposed to speaking)
- Problems sequencing and linking ideas and words in sentences, sentences in paragraphs and paragraphs in essays
- Limited and repetitive vocabulary
- Lack of knowledge of multiple meaning of words

2. Spelling and punctuation
- Problems with sequencing sounds in words in spoken and written language; especially noticeable in multisyllabic words and unfamiliar subject-specific words; Student often pronounces the word incorrectly and thus spells it incorrectly
- Continuing delay, even as adolescents, in establishing firm sound–symbol correspondence
- Confusion of words with similar sounds
- Difficulty identifying syllables in words
- Lack of understanding about boundaries between words and sounds within words
- Poor use of punctuation (thus making written work more difficult to read)

3. Organisation and planning
- Difficulty identifying themes, brainstorming, and summarising
- Limited output
- Work unplanned; writing poorly sequenced and confused
- Student unable to keep to the plan, even when plan is provided
- Student unable to articulate the purpose of a writing task; loses goal of writing easily
- Difficulty identifying major points and writing a topic sentence
- Difficulty getting started
- Difficulty bringing ideas together in a conclusion

4. Computer Skills
- Poor sound–symbol correspondence; inaccurate syllable count; inability to identify the correct word from a selection (all of which limit independent use of the spell-checker)
- Poor organisational skills affect ability to save and find files, and edit

5. Literate language skills (Adapted from Crystal (1979)).
- Poorly developed language to describe and identify genre
- Poorly developed language to describe and identify grammar
- Lack of subordinate clause structure – including subordinate conjunctions (because, when, while, since, although) and relatives (who, that, which)
- Limited use of literate conjunctions (when, since, before, after, while, because, so, as a result, if, until, but, therefore, however, although)
- Noun phrases, modifiers (old, wizened man) and qualifiers (for the afternoon) not elaborated upon

---

6. Grammar
- Frequent changing of personal pronouns and not establishing the referent for the pronoun
- Repetitive use of 'and' and 'then' in sentences
- Written work not always in complete sentences
- Verb–tense agreement troublesome

7. Comprehension
- Poor comprehension; limits quality and quantity of written language
- Difficulty understanding the formal language used in questions
- Written language not monitored from the reader's perspective
- Frequently fails to comprehend implied meaning in text; written responses are therefore confused and lack depth
- Problems with understanding and writing metaphors and similes; particularly noticeable in understanding and using images to write about emotions

8. Cognitive skills
- Difficulties making connections between events in a narrative
- Difficulties in connecting new knowledge to existing knowledge
- Difficulties with taking the point of view of others
- Difficulties in writing to a plan even when a plan is provided
- Poorly developed internal questioning and self-regulation makes independent editing, revising, and evaluation of written work difficult

9. Behaviour
- Holds faulty views about learning and especially writing
- Becomes frustrated and has difficulty in persisting
- Avoids written language tasks; sometimes related to feeling overwhelmed by written tasks that are perceived as being too big a task

M.Brent

Teaching genres

Finding a purpose

To help LLD students understand the purpose of different essay genres, connect each genre to keywords that explain the major features of each genre. It is also helpful to have good examples of each genre for students to read. Check students for comprehension and memory for each genre. Do not use too many words to explain the features of the different genres because too much language can be overwhelming for students with LLD.

Suitable keywords include the following:

- *narrative:* story, main event, entertaining (for example: fairy stories; historical events; Aesop's fables);

- *character study:* appearance, personality, actions;

- *instructional:* easy-to-understand steps, how to do/make something (for example: science experiments; recipes);

- *argumentative essay:* convincing people to agree with your point of view;

- *compare and contrast:* same/different, organise relevant themes and ideas;
- *analytical:* consider carefully, provide evidence or explanation.

Narrative plan

Once students understand the *purpose* of an essay genre, move onto a *very simple* plan and key topic words. Simple plans can seem rather prescriptive but some students will move on from these plans to develop their own plans over time. These simple plans can be used right up to fifth and sixth years to structure thoughts and ideas in students with LLD.

A suitable narrative plan is shown below.

Narrative plan

Purpose

A narrative tells a story. There is a main event and other events. The aim is to entertain the reader. Examples include novels, fairy stories, historical events, Aesop's fables.

Beginning

At the beginning of a narrative you need to answer the following questions:

- Where is the story taking place? You need to set the scene for the reader.
- Who are the main characters? Introduce these characters to the reader.
- When did the events take place?

Middle

In the middle of a narrative there is a complication or a problem.

End

At the end of the narrative the problem is solved (or 'resolved').

Check your work

When you finish your narrative check:

- Have you set the scene?
- Did you introduce the main characters?
- Have you sequenced your ideas?
- Is there a complication or a problem?
- Have you resolved the problem?

Teaching tips

Narratives

Some useful tips for teaching essay genres include the following.

- A good way to teach the narrative genre with older students is using Aesop's fables because they are short, easy to read and yet challenging enough to examine the sequence of beginning, middle and end, along with exploring themes and morals.

- Setting the scene for the reader can be extremely difficult for students and they might need further questioning to firm up their ideas.

- To expand students' vocabulary connect keywords to simpler words (for example, 'narrative' = 'story').

- Story boards can be very useful.
- Add in simple questions if necessary.

  Figure 10.9 shows some work on Aesop's fable *The Fox and the Grapes*.

Figure 10.9 Child's work on Aesop's fable

THE FOX AND THE GRAPES
This fable is about a fox trying to get some grapes but he can't reach them. The fable is saying that if people can't do something they either look for something to blame or just leave it.
An example of this is when I find work hard to do and just don't do it or I blame the teacher.

THE FOX AND THE GOAT
The fable is about a goat that goes down a well for a drink, but once he has had the drink he can't get back up. The fox comes along and tells the goat that he is a fool. This fable is saying that you should look before you leap. an example of this in my life would be when I was in cooking class and we were doing a recipe of chicken rosioto. I didn't read through the sheet before I started cooking and I totaly mucked up the chicken rosito. this is an example of "look before you leep".

Anonymous student (work published with permission of student)

Argumentative and analytical essays

Argumentative and analytical essays pose particular difficulties for LLD students. The following tips are suggested.

Generating questions and reflection

The underlying language disability makes it difficult for students to generate and sustain a high level of internal questioning and reflection. They need to start with very simple topics and require assistance in developing questions and sequencing their argument.

Summarising

Summarising can be difficult. Students might need to go back to keywords and ideas or themes. Summaries of texts are very helpful to give students an overview and to help with comprehension and the identification of themes

Editing

Students will require teacher assistance with the editing of their work, especially for grammar and meaning.

Formulating a point of view

Students might need help in formulating their own point of view and giving evidence for it. Significant preparation is necessary and participation in debating can be useful. If this is not feasible, involve students in planning points to be argued, and giving evidence to support them. This is another preteaching step in learning to write argumentative and analytical essays.

A suitable teaching plan for an argumentative essay is shown below.

Argumentative Essay Plan

Purpose
To persuade someone to your point of view (for example, newspaper opinion articles and editorials).

Keywords
[Supply appropriate key words here.]

Paragraph 1	State the topic. • What is the topic? • What is your point of view?
Paragraph 2	Give your reasons for your point of view. • Why do you think this? • What is your evidence?
Paragraph 3	Give opposing viewpoint • What is the opposing view? • Why is it not convincing?
Conclusion	Sum up. • Do you have a solution? • Give reasons for your conclusion.

A suitable teaching plan for an analytical essay is shown below.

Analytical Essay Plan

Purpose
To consider a topic carefully and provide evidence or explanation.

Introduction
• Provide a general statement of the subject area.
• Introduce the specific topic within the general subject.

Body
• Point 1 topic sentence, followed by evidence and quotes.
• Point 2 topic . . .
• Point 3 topic . . .

Conclusion
Link to topic stated in introduction.

The following analytical essay plan for *Tom Sawyer* takes the basic plan and adapts it for a specific novel. It provides the students with model paragraphs to get them started, as well as identifying the teacher's expectations (for example, key sentences, linking sentences, and quotations).

Figure 10.10 Analytical essay plan for *Tom Sawyer*

Tom Sawyer
Planning an Analytical Literary Essay

PART 1

Topic

Tom's life is a humorous and exciting one with many lessons to be learned.

How does Mark Twain show this to the reader?

Your essay must have an:

- introductory paragraph – this describes what your essay is about;
- body – this consists of several paragraphs; each paragraph supports the topic and must explain how Tom learns; begin each paragraph with a key sentence;
- concluding paragraph – this sums up what Tom learns briefly; you must mention the topic somewhere in the paragraph.

Sample essay

Introductory paragraph (example)

Annotation	Text
Mention the name of the main character	Tom Sawyer is the main character of Mark Twain's novel, <u>The Adventures of Tom Sawyer</u>. Aged about twelve, he lives with his Aunt Polly in St Petersburg, Missouri, in the 1840s. Life for Tom revolves around the small township and the Mississippi River. Early in the narrative we find that Tom can be described as a mischievous boy. Somehow he always manages to find himself in dangerous or amusing situations, where he is forced to use all his cunning to save himself. Despite the problems he creates and the punishment, Tom learns many lessons, not all of which take place in the classroom.
Give some background of family or setting or time	
Describe what the essay is about and use this link sentence to carry it through to the body of the essay.	

Mention the author and title of the book

Description of the main character and a little of the story's plot

Body

This consists of several paragraphs. Each paragraph supports the topic and must explain how Tom learns. Begin each paragraph with a key sentence.

Sample key sentences

When Tom is punished by Aunt Polly, and is given the chore to white-wash a long fence, he learns that by cunning, he is able to have others complete the task. (You then explain how Tom learned to manipulate others.)

A visit to a graveyard in the middle of the night creates many problems for Tom and his friends and he finds that this adventure, while proving to be exciting, creates many frightening situations in the months to come.

Tom learns many lessons about girls as he pursues Becky Thatcher.

Concluding Paragraph

This is a summing up of what Tom learns.

Be brief.

Somewhere in the paragraph you must mention the topic.

Advice

Try to include quotations and acknowledge them.

For example '...............................' page number.

When writing your draft essay, take a highlighter and colour in all the key sentences to make sure that they are there. Also colour all the items that must be in the introductory and concluding paragraphs.

Joan Rimer

Artwork analytical essays

The format for analysing a work of art is another example of an analytical plan. It is a highly prescriptive plan for use by senior students. This particular subject area requires specific vocabulary and terminology – and a suitable plan reflects this. The plan should show good examples of identifying keywords and provide heavy use of 'structure scaffolding' (which is necessary for LLD students). Such plans could be adapted for other subject areas that require subject specific vocabulary. For an example of such a plan, readers are referred to Lane & Darby (1998) – see references, page 131.

The following is an example of writing from a fifth year student with LLD, based on a poster. The student's initial attempts at writing were chaotic and disorganised and she could not write under timed conditions. Her words and ideas were repetitive and she tended to panic.

She was taught to write using two plans; a compare/contrast plan (for notes on this, see page 87) and an argumentative plan (for notes on this, see page 82) with topic sentences and keywords. Her plan is shown in Figure 10.11.

Because of her LLD, it was important that she write a simple sequenced plan with these keywords before starting to write under exam conditions. This helped her sequence her ideas and keep track of where she was in the essay. After 6–8 essays of this style she was able to produce the following example under exam conditions (Figure 10.12).

Figure 10.11 Student's plan for essay on JJJ poster

```
PLAN
Intro        •Age           - 14-18
             •Gender        - any both males + females
             •Purpose       - Advertise, Promote, Attract, Publicise, Inform
             •Audience      - General Public aimed at Adolescent teenagers

Design       •Line          - Js, cage, Thick black line
Elements     •Shape         - cage of Js
             •Tone          - background - sky blue - white
             •Colour        - bright and bold
             •Letter form   - Js are in the cage

Design       •Composition   - open
Principles   •Figure        - cage
             •Ground        - sky + mts
             •Cropping      - mts
             •Scale         - cage in large camera to trees + mts
             •Repetition    - Js, bricks, arms holding Js
```

Anonymous student (work published with permission of student)

Figure 10.12 Student's essay on JJJ poster

Did someone Say Sound Barrier?

Triple J is advertise there radio station which is aimed at teenagers, both males and females, aged around 14-18 years old. Triple J wants to attract more listeners and with this basic advertisement which is simple and strait to the point. Triple J is bracking all of the sound in music and you can do the same by tuning in to this station. You can see from the picutre the the triple (three) Js bracking out of the cadge. Where the Js have proken out the wire bars have bent to for there own Js which is quite unicue. The "sound barrier" is sertunly broken by triple J.

The line of the Js are seen throughout this advertisement. The black bold outline around all of the objects is clear and eyecatching.

Shape is present throughout the advertisement, with the cage being the main bold shape. All of the shaps are simple and easly drawn. This helps with the teenage evidence. Triple J has add there three basic Js in this advertisement with one flying away and two help back towards the by hands reinforcing the slogan.

The sky in the background has been tenderly rendered from a blue bold sky at the top and then moving down the page towards the hills becoming lighter and lighter until it hits a dusty white.

The colours in this advertisement are basic colours which are bold and vibrant. The black around each object helps the colour stand out and creates it as the figure.

The letter form of the company Triple J has been repped with the three 'J's breacking out of the cadge through the soond barrier. Where the 'J's have broken out the wire bares have formed there own 'J's.

This advertisement has an open copersion leating your eye look freely thrugout the advertisement.

The finger of the large cadge is eye catching and helps with the breacking of the Js through the sound barrier.

The ground of the sky and mts are soft and gental creating a pieceful envoroment.

The hills in the background at the bottom have been cropped and reduced in size, so they are not the main focal point, helping to create the cage as the focal point.

The hands have been skelled down so they are proportianly correct to the cadge. The tree and mt's are reduced in size so that the scale of the cage creats a eyecatch affect.

The repitition of the brics on the cadge helps creat a barrer affect with the hands reaching out to grab the Js. The hands have been reped with the top two catching two Js but the third flying away.

Triple J has created a advertisement which is clear and bold. The statement at the bottom is clearly represented by the cadge and the J's bracking through the sound barrier. Triple J is advertising a radio station which has the power to brack through the sound carrier and you two can do the same tune in!

Compare/contrast essay

Although the compare/contrast plan takes time to teach, it has enormous benefits for students. Through the lengthy brainstorming process, they have the opportunity to check their comprehension and attach this knowledge to key events and themes in the novel or argument.

Notes accompanying the other plans shown previously also apply to the compare/contrast plan.

Compare/contrast essay plan

Topic

Compare the characters of Miss Maudie and Aunt Alexandra in the novel *To Kill a Mockingbird.*

Brainstorm 1

- What do I know about Miss Maudie (consider physical appearance, interests, personality, opinions, relationship with key characters)?
- What do I need to find out?
- Where do I look in text or summary of text?

[Do the same for Aunt Alexandra.]

Brainstorm 2

How are Miss Maudie and Aunt Alexandra the same?

1. Characteristic: cooking skills
   - Miss Maudie: [fill in details]
   - Aunt Alexandra: [fill in details]
2. Characteristic: [another skill or characteristic]
   - Miss Maudie: [fill in details]
   - Aunt Alexandra: [fill in details]
3. Characteristic: [another skill or characteristic]
   - Miss Maudie: [fill in details]
   - Aunt Alexandra: [fill in details]

[Continue with other characteristics.]

Brainstorm 3

How are Miss Maudie and Aunt Alexandra different?

1. Characteristic: physical appearance
   - Miss Maudie: [fill in details]
   - Aunt Alexandra: [fill in details]
2. Characteristic: personality
   - Miss Maudie: [fill in details]
   - Aunt Alexandra: [fill in details]
3. Characteristic: relationship with Scout and Jem
   - Miss Maudie: [fill in details]
   - Aunt Alexandra: [fill in details]
4. Characteristic: understanding of people
   - Miss Maudie: [fill in details]
   - Aunt Alexandra: [fill in details]

[Continue with other characteristics.]

Introduction (beginning)

- Give title and author of book.
- Introduce the characters you are to contrast.
- Introduce main characteristics you will discuss (refer to brainstormed list).

> **Body (middle)**
> - 3–5 paragraphs
> - Begin each paragraph with a topic sentence using the characteristics or themes that you have identified in the brainstorming.
> - Use examples from the text to support your topic sentence.
>
> **Conclusion (end)**
> - Summary of contrast between characters
> - Your opinion

Instructional plan

Teaching tips for an instructional plan include the following.

Check comprehension

Check for comprehension and sequencing by asking an LLD student to explain the steps to another student or to the teacher. This step gives extra practice for students.

Correct language for the task

The language required when giving instructions is very subject-specific and students might, at first, attempt to use general language and gestures to explain the task. It is important to demand the correct language for the task.

Taking another's point of view

Taking the point of view of the reader is often very difficult for LLD students because of the high level of language skill required and the constant need to monitor their thinking with questions such as: Does this make sense? How could I make this clearer for the reader?

Organisation and sequencing

The organisation and sequencing difficulties of LLD become very obvious when following and writing instructions. Careful supervision is required because it is often very difficult for students to follow instructions sequentially. LLD students are tempted to miss steps.

Instructional essay plan

Purpose

The purpose is to provide clear instructions on how to do or make something (for example, science experiments; recipes; computer training manuals). This is done in clearly sequenced steps.

Materials	• How much? • How many? • List them in the order they are used.
Method	• Sequenced steps to get to goal • How? • With what? • Where?
Conclusion	• Your final concluding words on what was done.

Character study

Teaching tips for a character plan include the following.

Brainstorming

A character study can be a more difficult task than it might seem. Brainstorming key aspects of character and finding examples in the text can reveal significant gaps in comprehension.

Adjectives important

Students with poor vocabulary and expression might need to brainstorm adjectives to describe features and characteristics.

Use of quotations

Writing that includes quotations from the text is a very demanding linguistic task for LLD students because it involves matching the verb tense and vocabulary of the sentence to those of the quotation.

Identifying themes and topics

Main themes can be hard to identify. Teachers can use a compare/contrast plan to help identify these. The process of talking about similarities and differences between events and characters can help themes to emerge more clearly for students. Some students need assistance to develop topic sentences.

Character study

Purpose
To describe and analyse a particular person.

Instructions
Brainstorm words under the headings of:
- appearance;
- personality; and
- actions.

Introduction
- Name of text and author
- Main themes in text
- Briefly introduce the character

Body
- This consists of 4–5 paragraphs.
- Begin each paragraph with a topic sentence.
- The topic sentence should be about an aspect of the character's appearance, personality, or actions.
- Find examples in the text which prove your topic sentence.
- Use quotes from the text.

Conclusion
- Summary of the character (use ideas in topic sentences)

Newspaper reports

Teaching tips for newspaper reports include the following.

Importance of introduction

Students often confuse newspaper reporting with narrative writing. They need to understand the importance of putting all the most interesting and important information in the introduction, and that this must answer the questions: Who? What? When? Where? Why? How? Students need to identify the most important points first.

Body of report

Having written an introduction, students need to work on getting the report brief enough without losing the important points. When learning this genre students often put in too much detail and find difficulty in summarising while keeping all the important points.

Generating questions as part of the process

Remember that the inability to generate questions is part of the student's underlying language disability. Students need to understand the process of newspaper writing as an exercise in posing and answering questions.

Newspaper report

Headline	• Try to catch the attention of the reader.
Introduction	• Answer the questions: Who? What? When? Where? Why? How? • Include the most important and most interesting information. • Sentences should be short and simple, but interesting.
Body	• Add more detail. • Keep sentences and paragraphs short and simple.
Tail	• This consists of extra (but least important) information. • Includes a simple concluding statement.

Limitations in teaching students to write

Time and practice

Some LLD students might never move on from a prescribed formula in their writing and will continue to need a very structured approach with the basic plan provided by the teacher.

They also need longer to learn different genres. Such learning can take up to five months for each genre. LLD students need to write and revise eight essays for each genre, compared with two examples for other students (Wong, 1997). They also take longer to write, and they might not be able to complete the same number of written tasks as other students, nor complete them to the same complexity.

To help teachers and students set realistic timelines and amounts of work, it helps to have a clear idea of how long it will take students to learn a genre. If these tasks are completed in the classroom, teachers will have an accurate idea of the amount of time taken and effort needed. Thus they should provide a range of writing tasks and plans.

Reflecting on writing – polishing the end product

Once LLD students have finished a rough draft, they often do not want to continue to work on the piece. The notion that writing involves drafting and editing (to make ideas as clear as possible for the reader) eludes them. This is part of their language problem. The ability to ask and understand questions is often poorly developed in the oral language of LLD students. Thus they do not have the internal questions that more skilled writers use to monitor and edit their work. They do not ask themselves questions such as:

- Is this relevant to the topic?
- Could I use a different word?
- Does this make sense?

LLD students have significant problems in evaluating their work and making changes independently. Many students cannot tell if their grammar is incorrect or their meaning unclear, even if they read their work aloud. This is why conferencing with teachers is critical for problem writers (Wong, 1997). Conferencing forces students to think through their ideas and to examine the clarity of their expression. Conferencing is essential to improving comprehension and vocabulary.

To improve their written work, LLD students need to be able to identify their specific area of difficulty and be able to articulate that difficulty. For example:

- I need to make sure I understand the topic; or
- I have trouble getting enough vocabulary to write.

It is best if students come to this understanding during individual writing feedback sessions rather than in front of their peers.

A checklist of skills at each stage in the writing process can be useful in helping students to remember the steps in writing and to identify their areas of difficulty. The editing process needs another person and extra time. Cognitive and language skills can set limitations on the ability of LLD students to reflect on their writing.

To write or to type?

The use of computers is mandatory when teaching LLD students to write. With such students, the writing and editing processes typically involve a significant number of changes to be made to written work. Doing these by hand is time-consuming and discouraging.

If the handwriting of LLD students remains poorly developed by early secondary school, it is necessary to free them from the amount of concentration required for this motor task. This releases more cognitive energy to work on the processes of planning, reviewing, and editing.

Teachers should be alert for:

- slow writers with poor letter closure;
- students who cannot read their own writing;
- students who do not clearly separate the words when they write; and
- students who use a mixture of poorly formed printing and cursive writing.

Some resistance to using computers can be expected from LLD students because many have developed a 'busy' approach in general classrooms. We have found that LLD students routinely engage in endless rewriting of the same information, often directly copied from a text, without moving in any major way to the tasks of planning, summarising, editing, reorganising and reviewing their written work. Once the security of copying is removed, they initially feel very anxious as their specific areas of difficulty become more obvious.

Across the curriculum – meeting the needs of LLD students

A cross-disciplinary or cross-year approach is necessary with LLD students because of the number of skills to teach and the time needed to teach them. A school writing folder that is used over several years is a very useful tool. Ideally, this should contain:

- simple essay plans for different genres (English texts for Grades 5–8 often contain simple plans that can be used right up to sixth year);
- note-taking instructions and examples;
- good written models (from appropriate texts and peers);
- aids to comprehension (that is, background information that connects a topic to previous knowledge and one-page summaries of texts or films with key vocabulary and characters).

Conclusion

In a nutshell, in learning to write, LLD students need to:

- understand the purpose;
- comprehend the task and topic;
- brainstorm key words, ideas, and opinions;
- follow a basic plan;
- conference with the teacher; and
- have many opportunities to practise.

Assistance in mastering these skills will provide students with every opportunity to write to the best of their ability.

CHAPTER 11

School and Beyond – Skills to Help in Everyday Life

Introduction

Students with poor reading skills and other learning difficulties need to be taught skills that we often assume they know. Do not assume that the students will know how to do things. Rather, watch how they approach tasks to determine whether they are able to do them. Remember that adolescents who cannot perform the day-to-day tasks that their peers can perform become expert avoiders who can competently camouflage their difficulties. Start at the beginning and explain everything. The students might have missed important details and it is likely that they will be reluctant to reveal this by asking questions. Sometimes they do not know what questions to ask.

Some thoughts on teaching important life skills are discussed in this chapter.

Accessing computers

LLD students might not use computers as competently as their peers. Poor skills in spelling, reading and comprehension can make computer use very difficult. LLD students often make excuses *not* to use computers.

Students might not know how to solve problems they encounter and tend to resolve difficulties by closing up the computer and saying they have finished.

Teachers should be aware that students can be very reluctant to use computers and be prepared to persevere with encouraging and requiring students to use them.

Abigail wanted to go to the library to access more information from the Internet to complete her project. However, she was swamped with information and now needed to prepare the tables as required. When this next step became unavoidable, she first said that she did not have a disk. Then she said that she had done it on her computer at home and did not want to redo it. Pressed gently on the matter, she agreed that there were some sections that she had not done at home and that she could complete in the class.

▶

> With irritation she went and collected a laptop and disk and started working. She declined help, said that she was fine, and did not want to show the teacher how much she had done. Within ten minutes she closed the computer and said that she had finished. But she had not finished. She was unable to do the task as requested.
> A peer tutor was therefore arranged to show her what she needed to know, step by step.

Filling-in forms

Regular practice at filling-in forms might be necessary. The ability to give and write name, address, phone number, and date of birth must become an automatic response for students. This skill can be forgotten quickly if not repeated often.

Explanations are often required. For example, the notion that 'birthdate' and 'date of birth' are the same thing must be explained. Similarly, the meaning of 'next of kin' needs explanation for many students.

Forms that can be practised include the following:

- bank forms – including deposit and withdrawal forms, and cheques (especially the skill of writing numbers in words);
- health forms;
- application for membership forms – such as clubs, and so on;
- post office forms; and
- competition forms.

Reading and understanding labels

Reading and understanding labels are important in everyday life. Teaching these skills might require the use of models and samples of such things as:

- labels on foods;
- instructions and labels on medication; and
- safety and danger warnings.

With regard to the last of these, it should be noted that the word 'caution' is difficult to read and is unfamiliar to many students in everyday vocabulary. In addition, safety directions are often in tiny print and expressed in concise formal language. Examples of this formal language include:

- 'corrosive';
- 'avoid contact with eyes and skin';
- 'avoid breathing dust';
- 'do not mix with detergents or other chemicals';
- 'solution should be expelled from the mouth after use';

Students need explicit help in comprehending these sorts of formal instructions.

Banking

Electronic banking and use of EFTPOS are very common. Procedures for automatic teller machines (ATMs) vary among banks (and even among different types of machines of the same bank). Students need explanation and frequent practice with ATMs because information is entered in various ways and in different orders. Some banks have videos or pamphlets that can assist. Students also need to rehearse what to do if the machine does not work in the way expected.

Street directories

It is important for students to understand the information that is available within a street directory and to become familiar with its layout and organisation. Familiarisation with the front pages and organisation of a street directory is important because lots of essential information can be gleaned from them.

Useful skills include the following:

- alphabet skills (which might need to be revised);
- understanding symbols and landmarks;
- orientation for maps;
- use of grid references;
- areas of interest might need to be actually visited and looked at (for example, bike tracks or addresses of fellow students) to associate the directory information with the reality;
- abbreviations (such as 'St', 'Ave', and 'Rd') need explanation;
- attention to detail in addresses must be encouraged (for example, the differences among 'Smith Ave', 'Smith Crt', 'Smith Lane'); and
- teaching of strategies such as asking people to write addresses to ensure accurate spelling so that it is possible to look them up later in directories;

Telephone books

When teaching students to use telephone books, include the following:

- the use of *real* situations and the *real* phone book to look up genuine information (thus motivating students to learn to use the book);
- familiarising students with the layout of telephone books, where to find information and what 'directory assistance' means;
- looking up relatives and friends in the phone book;
- explanation of the arrangement of some common entries in directories (for example, whether or not government departments are listed under the name of the individual department or in a general listing of all government departments); and
- learning the different function and organisation of the 'Yellow Pages' (as opposed to the normal phone book) and practising such tasks as locating useful businesses (for example, the nearest bike shop).

Preparation for driving

Licence-testing now uses touch computer screens and learners' permits are available at the age of 16. Although touch screens are a 'friendly' method for many students, for others it can be difficult. One-to-one testing might be necessary for LLD students.

Some community centres have special courses (allied to adult reading classes). This is often an area in which students are interested and enthusiastic to learn.

Some useful ways to assist students are:

- learning the rules using toy cars (which can provide concrete examples of concepts such as 'giving way');
- flash cards for road signs;
- walking or driving the streets to identify signs and real-life situations; this is something that parents can do and considerable practice is necessary for automatic recognition and understanding to develop;
- licence-testing outlets might have other resource materials that can be of assistance; for example, videos, and these are useful because they can be replayed many times until students feel confident with the process.

Transport systems

Mastering the public transport system is very important for independence. Some students might be familiar with using trains, trams and buses, but others will not be confident or experienced. They need specific teaching and plenty of practice.

This could include:

- phoning for information for timetables;
- purchasing tickets from outlets or machines; learning how to validate tickets;
- attending to notices and signs, and understanding what they mean;
- understanding the structure of timetables and learning how to read them;
- the concept of alternative routes; and
- what to do when unexpected things happen (for example, catching the wrong train, having a bus not continue to its normal destination); these matters need to be well rehearsed because students will readily forget them in times of stress.

Preparing to enter the workforce

Moving from school into the workforce can be difficult for LLD students. Students have more success in jobs where employers take time to train them and where they can work on one task at a time. Students often manage better if they can attend work placements on a regular weekly basis for half a day, rather than for a block session of several days once a year.

Some areas that might require special attention are:

- learning to take instructions;
- learning strategies to compensate for their difficulties (for example, 'Could you say that again please?'; 'Can I check if I got that right?');
- recognising when they do not know, and learning how to seek help;
- seeing tasks through to completion;
- learning to answer the telephone;
- learning how to take messages and how to note all details; and
- practising how to ask for information and how to speak to customers.

There are many post-school options available for students and it is advisable to keep students informed about these throughout their years at secondary school. Encouraging students and their parents to consider realistic future options is important. Career planning is an area of growth and development. Government and private programmes are available to assist students in accessing further training and employment. Tertiary institutions have learning support staff members who can assist with course selection and who can assist students with their learning. There are also bridging programmes that combine school and work training. These all provide promising opportunities for LLD students.

It is essential that students in school be given assistance with planning for their futures. Without such support, making the transition into the workplace becomes extremely difficult. Studies show that if students are not given support, they are at high risk of remaining unemployed. Schools bear some responsibility for ensuring that students are prepared for life after school.

PART 3

Modifying the Curriculum

CHAPTER 12

Framework for Modifying Curriculum

Why modify curriculum?

Education today embraces the notion of catering for the learning styles and abilities of a wide range of students. The idea of 'teaching to the average' or teaching to a particular grade level is considered poor educational practice. The call for 'inclusive curriculum' connotes the idea that curriculum can be presented that will ensure the success of all students. This is a worthwhile ideal to attempt.

If students with LLD are to be successful, curriculum modification is essential. Curriculum modification can be seen as creating a 'by-pass', or using techniques to change the nature of the tasks presented to the students to reduce the negative effects of failure. Modification means changing the task to allow for successful and worthwhile learning. It requires forethought, flexibility, and consideration on the part of the teacher, and the support of school structure and policy. Classroom teachers might wish to modify work but there must be agreement within the school that the policy of modifying work is acceptable.

> Fairness means that everyone receives what he or she needs.
> Fairness does not mean that everyone receives the same.
>
> (Lavoie 1989)

The concept of curriculum modification is not always easy for school communities to accept. Although most teachers agree that it is important for all students to succeed, the question that is most often raised is: 'Is it fair to the other students?'.

For example, is it fair that:

- Mark has to do only two questions when other students have to do seven?
- Anna is not penalised for spelling errors when everyone else has been told that they will lose marks for spelling mistakes?
- John has someone to read him the questions in his test?
- Tracey does not have to write an essay on graffiti as everyone else has to do, but is required only to take photographs and ask a council worker some questions?

- Sam can ask questions in a test?
- Paul can do his test as an 'open-book test' whereas his classmates have been told that they cannot take notes into the test with them?
- Sarah does half an hour of maths homework and if she does not complete it all in that time she stops just the same?
- Elizabeth does not have to take the science test?

Teachers might feel uncomfortable about modifying curriculum (and, in particular, about modifying tests and test procedures) because they feel that they are:

- closing off options for students by not ensuring that they complete all aspects of the subject;
- professionally compromising and not doing their job properly;
- 'watering down' their subject area; and
- being unfair to other students.

A significant change of mindset is required to accept that individual difference requires broad curriculum development, curriculum modification, variable expectations and alternative evaluation. However, with modification, most students can achieve success.

Curriculum modification can involve:

- adjusting the *speed* at which information is presented and the speed at which responses are expected to be produced;
- adjusting the *amount* of work presented and expected;
- adjusting the *complexity* of the work presented and expected; and
- using *supportive* devices: computers, calculators, spell-checks, text-to-voice scanners, and checksheets.

How to modify curriculum

When modifying curriculum it is important to keep in mind a framework of skills or effective learning tasks that must operate across all subject areas. In other words, to modify curriculum in a worthwhile way, effective learning strategies as well as subject content must be considered.

It is important that all students learn to think and evaluate their learning at whatever stage and at whatever level they are capable of achieving. Teachers should have a clear idea of skills that are less demanding and skills that are complex. This is called a *hierarchy of learning skills*. Tasks can be modified in such a way as to give students experience with less complex skills as a foundation for later building more complex skills.

Figure 12.1 The Learning Wheel

The student:
- defines a problem for investigation
- independently clarifies the meaning of a research task using reference sources to clarify understanding
- states what is required when asked to devise a survey, debate, discuss, argue, investigate, compare and contrast, and identify positive and negative influences
- develops focus questions appropriate to the tasks and clusters focus questions under headings or subheadings
- prepares a search strategy in a standard format that incorporates the above information and that indicates types of sources suited to the task; understanding of the purpose and coverage of different types of resources should be demonstrated.

The student:
- follows and modifies a search plan
- pre-determines the appropriate resources for a topic recognising when sources external to the library are required
- identifies and locates resources:
  - using both single and combined terms
  - choosing broader or narrower terms in response to inadequate search results
  - eliminating inappropriate resources using information from the catalogue record
  - searching menu-driven external on-line databases and electronic information services
- locates, when appropriate, resources representing a range of viewpoints
- selects resources by surveying all aspects of a resource including recognising the significance of extended references, cross-references, and subtopics in an index
- uses specialist reference materials as directed
- uses a range of equipment to access information including on-line databases and CD-ROM.

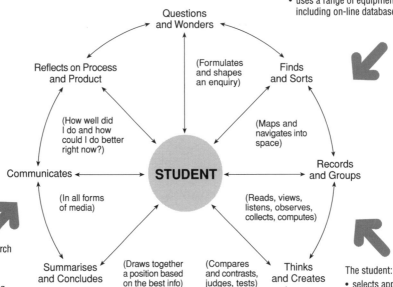

The student:
- creates a response to a research task that:
  - links ideas coherently
  - presents a position, making some attempt to justify ideas where appropriate
  - demonstrates limited ability to consider multiple viewpoints
  - uses some subject-specific words and phrases
- presents information using a form and organising framework selected with assistance to suit the purpose, audience, and information.
Included are:
  - written expositions, reports, summaries, procedures, descriptions, and explanations
  - oral reports, graphic, pictorial and dramatic presentations of similar complexity to the written presentations
  - constructions requiring syntheses and interpretation of information.

The student:
- discards irrelevant information after reviewing the purpose of the task
- evaluates and compares information from various sources for accuracy, omission, and bias
- synthesises information to make and substantiate judgments and to construct generalisations
- draws inferences from evidence
- arranges information collected in a logical coherent way, for example with headings and subheadings that are modified to suit the information gathered
- selects a format and framework suited to the task, information and audience
- modifies a standard framework to facilitate the logical coherent organisation of information to support the position being taken
- recognises information deficiencies and gathers specific additional information.

The student:
- selects appropriate information from a variety of sources including exhibitions, excursions, audio and visual recordings, and interviews by:
- using text context clues such as text headings and subheadings
- identifying main and subordinate areas modifying skimming and scanning techniques to suit text structure of source
- asking specific questions:
  - re-reading, re-listening and re-viewing
- records information by:
  - devising own note-making strategies
  - modifying note-making formats as appropriate to task and source
- considers a range of viewpoints by:
  - recognising whether information is closer to fact or opinion
  - identifying authority, purposes, and intended audience of source
- records source of information using author, title, date and place of publication, publisher, or alternative as appropriate.

Loertscher, David. (1996), *All That Glitters May Not be Gold*, reprinted with permission of *Emergency Librarian* (now *Teacher Librarian: the Journal for School Library Professionals*, Vol. 24, no. 2)
Notes around wheel: unpublished document from Department of Education, Western Australia

A framework of skills – the Learning Wheel

Effective learners think about their thinking. That is, they develop skills and strategies that they apply to their learning, and they reflect on their thinking processes. The Learning Wheel (Figure 12.1) helps to break down learning into a hierarchy of skills. We have used the School Library Association of Victoria's booklet *Using the CSF to Teach Information Skills* to isolate a number of skills that equip students well for learning and that should be taught.

It is unrealistic to expect that all students with LLD can be taught total proficiency and independence in each of these areas, but this framework can be used to identify skills that can be taught (in a modified form for some students). This learning provides a solid foundation upon which more complex skills can develop and allows teachers to value subskills that students learn in the course of completing assignments.

Learning skills – from simpler to more complex

Using the framework provided by the Learning Wheel (Figure 12.1), teachers can initially give tasks (or parts of tasks) that are simpler – to ensure that students can complete these – before moving on to more complex tasks. The wheel works by starting at the beginning of the process, 'Questions and Wonders', and moving around to 'Reflects on Process and Product'. However, it is not simply a linear process. There is room for moving backwards and forwards through the levels to make sure that tasks are completed satisfactorily.

1. Questions and Wonders

See the Learning Wheel (Figure 12.1). The first part of the wheel is 'Questions and Wonders'.

Can students turn a topic into a question to research? For example, a topic such as 'extinct animals' can be turned into a question such as: 'Why aren't there any more dinosaurs?'.

Do students understand the key terms in a task they are given such that they know what they have to do? For example, do they understand terms such as: 'describe', 'investigate', 'make notes on', 'discuss', 'compare', and 'contrast'? Some tasks are more complex than others. For example, 'describe' is easier than 'compare and contrast'.

Consider a task such as: 'Write about the lifestyles of Native Americans and Australian Aborigines'. Students can be assisted to pose questions about the lifestyles of the two groups. What were their houses like? What was their family life like? What did they eat? How did they collect their food? And so on. A teacher could then model a format by setting up a 'compare and contrast' grid.

Table 12.1 Compare and contrast grid

	Native Americans	Australian Aborigines
Housing		
Food		
Tools		
Lifespan		
Food-gathering		

To compare and contrast the lifestyle of Native Americans and Australian Aborigines, students need to find similar features and different features. The teacher could model this by asking specific questions, such as: 'Find two things the same and two things different about American Indians and Australian Aborigines'.

When given an assignment, LLD students often do not know what to do to begin the task. Teachers can help students develop key skills in various ways.

- They can help by brainstorming the topic (see 'Brainstorming', Chapter 10, page 72).

- Teachers can model and verbalise the thinking process in the following way. 'OK, I have to do some research. I have to find out something about extinct animals. No one has told me exactly what to find out so I can choose. Am I sure that I know what 'extinct' means? Yes, 'extinct' means . . . and I know about lots of animals that are extinct. There are woolly mammoths, dodos, and dinosaurs. It's hard to imagine a world full of dinosaurs. If I think about dinosaurs being so big and strong, its hard to know why they died out. I wonder what made them disappear?'

- Teachers can model brainstorming and can devise questions as part of a group. LLD students can share questions with other students and, with practice, can apply this experience to future investigations. (See example in Chapter 10, page 73.)

- Teachers can use a whiteboard to write up ideas and can then colour group issues that are related (see 'Mindmaps' in Chapter 8, page 47).

- Teachers can work out a broad plan of action after devising the question.

Teachers generally go through processes such as these with their classes. LLD students in a larger group cannot always benefit as much as we would like from these activities. This is because of the pace of presentation, the students' need for more explanation, and their need for someone to clarify links. Preteaching is helpful, thus allowing students to benefit more from the group interaction (see 'Preteaching', Chapter 6).

2. Finds and Sorts

Moving on to the next stage in the wheel (Figure 12.1), the stage of 'Finds and Sorts' involves locating information on the topic and sorting it.

Can students work out where information can be found?

Perhaps the information can be found in the library, in databases, on the Internet, or in other places. Can they devise search terms on their given topic and follow menu-driven databases? LLD students might not read databases easily, not attend to them, or not interpret them correctly. Do they know that new search terms might produce better results if the first one fails to yield suitable material? Can they come up with new search terms? (See Chapter 8, Libraries and Research, page 44, for more on these matters.)

LLD students can be proficient at locating information if they are good visual processors, if they are good organisers, and if they have competence in practical areas. For some it is an area of great strength. However, often the abilities of LLD students in this area are patchy. Some students avoid these tasks, others rely on group dynamics, and others download large slabs of material containing words they recognise. (See 'Dealing with information', page 44, for strategies to assist with this problem.) Working in groups can be an appropriate way to support LLD students but teachers need to ensure that there are opportunities for students to practise these skills independently.

To encourage 'finding and sorting', a modification to the assignment on 'extinct animals' (this chapter, page 104) could be that students locate information, print or photocopy it, and highlight sections that are relevant to the question – rather than producing a lot of writing. The emphasis is then on the skill of 'finding and sorting' – rather than on writing skills (which can be developed at a later stage when 'pre-writing' skills have been attained).

Can students identify suitable information?

Can students identify information that they can read and understand, and reject other material? It is common for LLD students to download anything that the database identifies as related to their search – whether or not they can read and understand it.

Can students recognise that information can differ?

Can students recognise that different sources might have different information on the same topic? See Figure 12.2.

Figure 12.2 Facts can vary from different sources

The Wreck of the *Batavia*					
Amazing Australian Shipwrecks	*The Australian Encyclopaedia*	*The Concise Oxford Dictionary of Australian History*	*The Macquarie Book of Events*	*Before the First Fleet*	*Western Australia: Home of the America's Cup*
What date did the *Batavia* leave Holland?					
28 March 1628	28 October 1628	October 1628			October 1628
How many soldiers, crew, and passengers were on board?					
316		300		268	268
What date did the *Batavia* run onto a reef?					
4 June 1628	4 June 1628	June 1629	4 June 1629	1629	4 June 1629 [p.45] 1619 [p.45]
Which Dutch captain were these islands named after?					
					Frederik de Houtman
How many kms off the WA coast are these islands?					
50 km	70 km	75 km		64 km	60 km [p.45] 70 km [p.29]

Sue Healey

Faced with this sort of variation, students can be encouraged to make up a table setting out differences clearly. For example, faced with different information on the extinction of dinosaurs, students could produce the following sort of table.

Table 12.2 Grid for variation in information

Question	Book A	Book B	Book C
Why did dinosaurs die out?	A meteorite hit the earth and killed them.	The temperature warmed up and they couldn't adjust.	Food ran out.

Can students skim and scan to find relevant material efficiently?

The ability to skim through material looking for key words and phrases is an important skill that can be taught and practised.

3. Records and Groups

Moving on to the next stage in the wheel (Figure 12.1), the stage of 'Records and Groups' involves organising and recording information.

Can students record information?

Students must be able to record information. This can be in words, in their own shorthand, or in graphics. They must, of course, be able to understand it again later.

Can students sort information?

Students can use index cards with the questions written on the top and, as they obtain relevant information, write it beneath the questions on the cards. Or students can devise or use a notetaking sheet in grid form to group and record the information. (See 'Standard of Ur', Chapter 9, page 53.) If several sources are being used, each can be written in a different colour. For some students, completing this might be an appropriate modification of a larger task and will teach important skills to aid thinking and comprehension. These skills can be further developed.

Can students develop headings and subheadings?

LLD students often require help in developing appropriate headings and subheadings under which they can organise the material they have collected.

Can students differentiate between fact and opinion?

Students might find (or be given) some information and then be asked to highlight facts in one colour and opinions in another. Alternatively, they can be asked to produce a table with the same differentiation between fact and opinion.

Can students record sources of their information?

The recording of sources can be demonstrated and students can be given examples. Recording information from different sources in different colours is good preparation for this.

4. Thinks and Creates and 5. Summarises and Concludes

Moving on to the next two stages in the wheel (Figure 12.1), we come to 'Thinks and Creates' and 'Summarises and Concludes'.

These involve the following sorts of questions:

- Can students select suitable information and reject information that is not suitable?
- Can students present information in a logical way with headings?
- Can students go and find more information if all areas are not covered?
- Can students put together the information as a final point of view or conclusion?

6. Communicates

The next stage in the wheel (Figure 12.1) is 'Communicates'.

Today there is a host of ways in which work can be presented and it is important that students are familiar with a range of them. These might include posters, graphics, PowerPoint, and webpages. Many of the electronic formats allow information to be presented in dot points and for links to be demonstrated by the click of a button. This is generally much easier for LLD students as it saves lengthy writing and difficulties with expression. If confidence is an issue, some work can be presented in note form or orally (perhaps to the whole class, or to a small group, or even to the teacher alone).

7. Reflects on Process and Product

The final stage in the wheel (Figure 12.1) involves reflection on the process and the product.

It is important for learning that students think about what they have done. Providing areas to consider in the form of criteria sheets is helpful for many tasks. Simple criteria sheets can be used to check off each stage of the task. Or they can be designed to encourage students to consider their approach to the steps in the task.

Criteria sheets can take several forms. A detailed example is shown in Figure 12.3.

Figure 12.3 English criteria assessment sheet

English Criteria Assessment Sheet

Quest Story

Name:	Date:			
	High	Medium	Low	Not Shown
Ability to sustain a creative and interesting point				
Ability to develop characters				
Introduction, opening line/s – the ability to capture the audience's attention				
Evidence of editing and proofreading				
Correct use of spelling and grammar				
Structures (that is, paragraphing)				
Language and expression				
General Comments				
Grade				

Karyn Murray

Conclusion

The Learning Wheel provides a useful model for curriculum modification. It can be used as a way to consider the complexity of skills needed for effective learning. Each level interacts with others in a way that encourages students to re-evaluate what they are learning and producing.

Teachers can use the Learning Wheel to determine the levels of tasks given to students and can use it to produce modifications for students experiencing difficulties. Teachers can also use the Learning Wheel as a framework to substitute simpler tasks for LLD students when the tasks expected of other students are too complex.

In this way they are encouraging worthwhile learning in students who cannot complete the whole task.

LD students have difficulty generating vocabulary and
cause difficulties in getting started on the research process.
ent their feeling overwhelmed by the task, it is important to
skills slowly. There are additional steps that can be added
udents confront text.

PLANNING
REASONING
REFLECTING

CHAPTER **13**

How to Modify the Amount of Work

Students often feel overwhelmed when presented with a page of tightly worded text. Even when they are capable of doing all the tasks presented, they can panic – simply at the 'look' of the task.

Assignment presentation

Presenting assignments in an appropriate way can be crucial to the way in which they are completed. Some extra time spent on layout, design, and the way that the questions are worded can significantly influence the quality of work produced by students. This is true of all the students in the class, not just those with LLD. Some important things to remember are noted below.

Layout

Take care with the layout of assignments. It is essential that they are presented with the following points in mind.

Typed

Assignments should be typed because typed information is much easier to read than handwritten information.

Uncluttered

Uncluttered assignments are easier to comprehend. It can help if lines are one-and-a-half or double-spaced because this can reduce the anxiety some students experience when faced with a full page of text with little white space. Underlining should be kept to a minimum.

Not too 'wordy'

Questions should be kept short and to the point.

Clear in page layout

Try to be consistent from assignment to assignment, using similar font and layout (for example, 'aims' and 'date due'). Consistent layout reinforces what students need to do. Use a minimum point size ('type size') of 10 and a clear font style (Arial, Comic Sans).

Steps or sections

Indicate how the task can be broken down into separate steps or sections. Go through the whole assignment with the students to give an overview of the whole task and then allocate it one section at a time. Remember that LLD students might need to go over the assignment several times.

Timeline

Give a timeline for completing each section and monitor this. You might put in a check box and date for each section.

Figure 13.1 Presenting information clearly

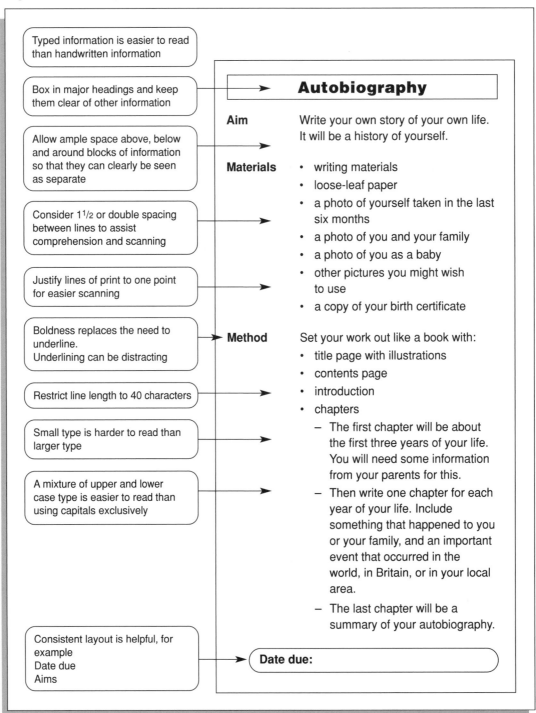

Brent, Gough and Robinson 1988

Time considerations

LLD students are slow to complete work. This can be for a variety of reasons, including the following:

- they might be slow to understand the task and require explanations to comprehend;
- they might read slowly;
- they might have difficulty interpreting information accurately;
- they might be slow in forming answers;
- they might be disorganised;
- they might need to seek assistance often; and
- they might take longer with editing and checking.

Teachers often underestimate the length of time it takes LLD students to complete their work. It takes LLD students approximately three times as long to complete assignment work at home as it takes in class.

Teachers should actually observe students at work and gauge the time it takes them to complete tasks. It is important to check when students report that they have completed work – to be sure that they have completed all parts of the task with the detail required.

Assignments should be designed to accommodate both simplification and extension. Negotiate with students which sections they can complete within the necessary timeframe. For example, students might be asked to research and present a report on the ways in which a water animal, a land animal and a flying animal are variously adapted to their environment. LLD students might be asked to research only one of these. Alternatively, they might be asked to research two animals but allowed to present their work in note or poster form rather than being required to present a report.

In general, teachers can arrange work in sections and require that all core sections be done, with further sections being completed with negotiation.

Teachers can reduce the amount of work by:

- providing some of the information;
- providing one of the articles for study and have students find one more;
- selecting articles from a collection to reduce search time;
- providing cloze sheets rather than have students write paragraphs;
- preparing a 'proforma' for students to complete – rather than requiring them to write up the whole task by themselves;
- using such a proforma to model how to do parts of the task that students might not be sure of (for example, when asked to 'record data and write a conclusion', students often look blank because they simply do not know what is required of them);

- requiring paragraph responses rather than essay responses;
- adapting the amount of work to be done but keeping a similar task format; and
- allowing students to present their information pictorially or diagrammatically (for example, using annotated timelines instead of essays, or representing the lifecycle of an insect pictorially, rather than describing this in words).

Some examples of modifications

Cloze activities

The following are examples of cloze activities for science.

The first example (Figure 13.2) allows students to learn the vocabulary of solutions without having to write large amounts.

The second (Figure 13.3) is a proforma that is modified but which corresponds with the textbook. It models data entry and the structure of a report with direct reference to the textbook, and the conclusion is a cloze activity.

The third example (Figure 13.4) is less modified. Students write their own aims and conclusions.

Figure 13.2 Cloze activities, example 1

Complete the passage below by using words in the box. Take care!

Solutions

When you stir _____ in a cup of tea, it seems to _____ into the water. We say the sugar dissolves or is _____ in the water. The sugar and _____ have formed a solution. A _____ is a special mixture in which a solid substance (the sugar) _____ in a liquid (the water). Solutions might be coloured, but they are always _____. You can see through them. The solid that dissolves is called the _____ (the sugar). The _____ that does the dissolving is called the solvent (the water). So the solute (the sugar) dissolves in the _____ (the water), forming a solution. The solute is spread _____ through the solvent. The parts of a liquid solution do not separate to form a sediment.

Dissolving is not the same as melting. In melting you turn a solid into a liquid by heating, for example melting ice to water.

(sugar, dissolves, solution, disappear, water, solute, evenly, clear, soluble, liquid, solvent)

Diane Grochowska

Figure 13.3 Cloze activities, example 2

Getting and Storing Energy

Heinemann Book 2 Chapter 6.1

Peanut Power –

Aim: To determine the amount of energy that can be obtained from the burning of a peanut.

Materials: See page 81 Heinemann Book 2.

Method: See page 81 Heinemann Book 2.

Result:

Peanut	Weight	Start	Finish	Difference	Sum	Energy(J)
e.g.	0.5g	15 C	60 C	45 C	45*42J=	1890 J
1.					__*42J=	
2.					__*42J=	
3.					__*42J=	
4.					__*42J=	
5.					__*42J=	

Total of energy column = _____

Now divide the total number by 5 to get an average energy value for a peanut.

Sum: _____ = _____ joules.

Conclusion:

Use the words in the box to complete the sentences below.

tissues joules worn peanut energy foods

Heat and other forms of energy are measured in _____.

When a _____ burns it releases _____.

The average amount of energy a peanut releases is _____.

We use energy from _____ to do everyday activities, build new _____ and repair _____ and damaged tissues.

Diagram:

Adaptation by Diane Grochowska of Parsons, M. (1996).
Heinemann Outcomes Science 2, Rigby Heinemann, Melbourne, p. 81.

Figure 13.4 Cloze activities, example 3

Getting and Storing Energy

Heinemann Book 2 Chapter 6.1

Peanut Power –

Aim: _____

_____

Materials: See page 81 Heinemann Book 2.

Method: See page 81 Heinemann Book 2.

Result:

Peanut	Weight	Start	Finish	Difference	Sum	Energy(J)
e.g.	0.5g	15 C	60 C	45 C	45*42J=	1890 J
1.					__*42J=	
2.					__*42J=	
3.					__*42J=	
4.					__*42J=	
5.					__*42J=	

Total of energy column = _____

Now divide the total number by 5 to get an average energy value for a peanut.

Sum: _____ = _____ joules.

Conclusion:

_____

_____

_____

_____

_____

_____

_____

Diagram:

Adaptation by Diane Grochowska of Parsons, M. (1996).
Heinemann Outcomes Science 2, Rigby Heinemann, Melbourne, p. 81.

Maths assignment

Sam's teachers were pleased with his attitude to homework. It was always completed and correct.

But Sam's mother reported that everyone in the neighbourhood helped with his homework. It was too difficult for him. By the time that they found someone who could help him complete it, it was always late and there had been many frustrated tears.

No one at school knew how much time and effort went into completing homework.

Simple changes can make a great difference to students who are experiencing difficulties at school. Sam's life (as well as his mother's) could have been made far less stressful with simple reductions in the amount of work that was required of him. Such a reduction in demands would also have taught Sam the valuable lesson of completing a task.

The following is an example of an original maths assignment (Figure 13.5). It is followed by the modification (Figure 13.6).

Figure 13.5 Original maths assignment

Year 7 Measurement Project

Name: _____ Due Date: _____

Each part of this project deals with different aspects of the measurement topic. After discussion in class, you should attempt to complete each section **promptly** then tick the box on the criteria sheet. Remember to have your project **signed** and submit the criteria sheet with your project.

PART 1: Personal details

1. Using the most appropriate instruments, take the following measurements of yourself:
   a) height
   b) weight
   c) handspan (with outstretched fingers)
   d) foot length
   e) armspan (with outstretched arms)
   f) head circumference (around forehead)
   g) wrist circumference

Using either a photo or sketch of yourself, indicate your measurements with arrows to the relevant parts. Remember to **include all units**.

2. Find the area of your hand by tracing it onto graph paper and counting squares. Show all working and include the graph sheet.

3. Find the length of your normal walking pace and running pace by taking 10 paces and measuring the distance covered, then calculate the average length of each pace. Show all calculations.

4. Now use your personal details above to **copy and complete**:

   a) The number of paces I would take to run 1 mile is approximately _____
   b) The heaviest pumpkin grown weighed 351.3 kg. This is approximately _____ times my weight.
   c) The largest dinosaur was reported to be 5.9 metres tall. This is approximately _____ times my height.

---

d) The largest crab found had a claw span of 3.7 metres. This is approximately ___ times my armspan.

e) The regulation height of a tennis net is 915 mm. This is about ____ times my handspan. The area occupied by 1 square metre is approximately ___ times the area of my hand.

f) Ian Thorpe's feet are 36 cm long. My foot is approximately _____ (write a fraction) the length of his foot.

Figure 13.6 Modified maths assignment

Year 7 Measurement Project

Name: _____ Due Date: _____

Each part of this project deals with different aspects of the Measurement topic. The project will be handed out in separate parts and you should note the due date for each part. After discussion in class, you should **promptly** complete that section of the project and **tick the boxes on criteria sheet**. Remember to have each part of your project **signed**.

PART 1: Personal details

1. Complete the following table of your personal details using the most appropriate measuring instruments. Remember to include all units.

a) height	
b) weight	
c) handspan (with outstretched fingers)	
d) foot length	
e) armspan (with outstretched arms)	
f) head circumference (around forehead)	
g) wrist circumference	

2. Find the area of your hand.
   Trace your hand onto graph paper and count the squares.
   Show all working and include the graph sheet in your project.

3. Find the length of your normal walking pace and running pace.
   Take 10 paces and measure the distance covered.
   Calculate the average length of each pace.
   Show all calculations in this table:

Walking	Running
Length of 10 paces =	Length of 10 paces =
Average length of one pace =	Average length of one pace =

4. Now use your personal details to complete these statements:

   a) To walk 1 mile, I would take approximately _____ paces.

   b) To run half a mile, I would take approximately _____ paces.

   c) The heaviest pumpkin grown weighed 351.3 kg. This is approximately _____ times my weight.

   d) The largest dinosaur was 5.9 metres tall. This is approximately ____ times my height.

e) The largest crab found had a claw span of 3.7 metres. This is approximately ___ times my armspan.

f) The regulation height of a tennis net is 915 mm. This is about ____ times my handspan.

g) The area of this A4 sheet of paper is _____ . This is approximately ____ times the area of my hand.

h) Ian Thorpe's feet are 36 cm long. My foot is approximately _____ (write a fraction) the length of his foot.

Criteria sheet

Tick	Criteria					
	PART 1 1a–g Personal measurements including units					
	2 Area of hand					
	3 Length of walking and running pace					
	4a–h Completion of statements					

History assignment

Modifications can also be made to history projects. See the original assignment (Figure 13.7) and compare with the revised version shown in Figure 13.8.

Figure 13.7 Original history assignment

The Changing Role of Women
Major Research Assignment

Name: _____

Aims
- To identify the changes to women's traditional roles in the twentieth century.
- To study the way women worked together to achieve these changes.
- To encourage students to use a computer to present historical information.

Topic
'Working Together : The Changing Role of Women in the Twentieth Century'

Assignment instructions

Method
Synthesise your information into a report which puts across your point of view both visually and in written form.

Support your opinions with primary visual evidence.

Presentation
Choose from the following methods of presenting the report:

An annotated visual display (documents, pictures, photos, tables, and graphs) with a written report giving explanations of the visual material showing the changing role of women and how this change was achieved.

OR

A newspaper article which gives a commentary and point of view about the changing role of women and the ways women achieved this. Your article must include visual information that explains and supports your commentary and opinion.

Note

- All documents, pictures, photos, graphs, tables are to be fully annotated (labelled).
- All presentations require a bibliography to be submitted.
- Students are encouraged to use computer technology where possible. (Desk top publishing/print shop, scanning etc.)
- Time will be allocated in class and in the library for research and for using computers.

Assignment Instructions

You are to research the topic in detail by choosing ONE of the following areas:

EITHER

1914–1945 World War I, The Great Depression & World War II

To help guide your research, answer the following:

- How did World Wars I and II alter traditional roles of women?
- During both wars, what kind of employment did women have? What was society's attitude to women working?
- What was the role of women in the nursing service?
- Why was the Women's Land Army important to the role of women?
- What did women do on the Home Front?
- What kinds of employment were women able to find after World War I and World War II?
- How did the Great Depression affect women? Did this period set the women's movement back? Why?
- What was the 'Women's Peace Movement'; and why was it important to the struggle for women's opinions to be heard?
- Did women work together in all these areas?

OR

The Women's Movement/Women's Liberation Movement 1950s–1970s

To help guide your research, answer the following:

- After World War II what role did women play in the workforce?
- What demands did women make after 1948 for freedom of choice in education, careers, working conditions, marriage, and families?
- How did the fight for equal pay after World War II change the role of women?
- In what areas did women enter the public sphere (that is, outside the family)?
- How did this result in the fight to remove discrimination against women? Look for examples in politics, employment, commerce, business, the law, academic studies, sport, the arts.
- Who were the leaders in the Women's Liberation Movement?
- How was the fight undertaken? Did women work together?

Why did this movement change the role of women so dramatically?

Date due:

Andrea Turner, History Department, Tintern AGGS

Figure 13.8 Revised history assignment

The Changing Role of Women
Major Research Assignment

Name: _____

Aims

- To identify the changes to women's traditional roles in the twentieth century
- To study the way women worked together to achieve these changes
- To encourage students to use a computer to present historical information

Topic

'Working Together : The Changing Role of Women in the Twentieth Century'

Assignment instructions

Method

Present your information in a report that includes written and visual information.

Support your information with primary visual evidence.

Presentation

You have a choice of two ways to present your report:

1. An annotated visual display that might include documents, pictures, photos, tables, and graphs. This must also have a written report that gives explanations of the visual material. This information must show the changing role of women and how this change was achieved.

2. Present a newspaper article that gives a commentary and point of view about the changing role of women and the way that women achieved this. Your article must include visual information that explains and supports your commentary and opinion.

Note

- All documents, pictures, photos, graphs, tables are to be labelled (annotated).
- All presentations require a bibliography to be submitted.
- Students are encouraged to use computer technology where possible (for example desktop publishing, print shop, scanning etc.).
- Time will be given in class and in the library for research and for using computers.

Task

Research in detail

The Women's Movement/Women's Liberation Movement 1950s–1970s

Answer the following questions

- After World War II what role did women play in the workforce?
- How did the fight for equal pay after World War II change the role of women?
- In what areas did women enter the public sphere (that is, outside the family)?
- How did this result in the fight to remove discrimination against women? Look for examples in politics, employment, commerce, business, the law, academic studies, sport, the arts.
- Who were the leaders in the Women's Liberation Movement?
- Write a paragraph to answer the question 'Did women in the 50s–70s make any gains?'.

Florence Gough

CHAPTER **14**

How to Modify the Complexity of Tasks

Introduction

When setting tasks for LLD students it is important to keep in mind that some tasks are easier than others. For example it is easier to 'describe' than it is 'to compare and contrast'. It might not be necessary to modify all tasks.

The way that language is used in a task can be vital. Teachers should be careful about the language that they use. They should try to use straightforward language that is easy to understand. 'Literate language' (the language of textbooks) has a particular style that is more difficult to understand. Teachers can change this language to make the task easier. The following example was found in an assignment for second year students.

> . . . this unit is designed to give you maximum flexibility whilst still maintaining a compulsory core. Certain tasks will have to be done together as class exercises but otherwise you will be able to work at your own pace as long as you complete the required number of tasks in the given time . . . It is your responsibility to ensure that tasks are satisfactorily completed and submitted.

This could be rewritten as:

> This unit has been planned so that you can make choices about what you do.
> Some tasks you *must* complete as class activities.
> Other tasks you can choose yourself from the lists in each section.
> You will have to organise your own time so that you complete all your work and hand it in by the due date.

Another example from a textbook reads as follows:

> In many countries drinking water is recovered by separation from sea water which is too salty to drink. Two separation techniques must be used to achieve the recovery of pure water. They are . . .

This can be modified to read:

> Many countries make drinking water from sea water.
> Salt must be taken out of sea water (separated from the water).
> There are two steps (techniques) that must be used to take salt out of sea water.
> These are . . .

Some ideas for modifying complexity

The modifications to the examples above are relatively simple, but they can make an enormous difference to the approach and attitude that LLD students have towards required tasks.

Some of the ways in which teachers can modify the complexity of tasks are noted below.

Clear written instructions

Give clear written instructions with all tasks. Remember that students might not understand or remember all the details. Remember also that other people might be helping students and will need to know how to help with the task.

Purpose and steps

Write instructions in a way that makes clear the purpose of the assignment and the order in which steps should be completed. If necessary, state what needs to be done first, second . . . and last. This structure can help LLD students find direction when they are not sure what they should be doing next.

Levels of difficulty

Provide assignments and tasks that have a range of levels of difficulty. Adolescents like to have the opportunity to exercise choice, so several suitable options are a good idea. However, at times, choice should be restricted so that students do not make an inappropriate selection.

Resources

Liaise with library staff to ensure that a range of resource materials is available – including picture books, posters, books (of varying complexity), magazines, and so on. Remember that pictures can be a valuable source of information. (See, for example, the 'Standard of Ur', page 53.)

Interviews

Consider setting assignments in which students obtain information from interviews with real people.

Student presentation options

To reduce the need for extensive writing, consider different ways in which students might present work – including graphic presentation, PowerPoint and posters.

LLD students generally do better when the amount of reading and writing is reduced. Give alternatives in presenting work such as:

- group responses in which LLD students are responsible for part of the work;
- poster presentations;
- illustrative and graphic presentations;

- oral presentations to the teacher alone or to a small group (if presenting to the whole class is daunting);
- video presentation;
- shorter written responses (for example, writing a paragraph rather than an essay, or completing a cloze activity instead of writing a paragraph).

Specific instructions

Consider altering research tasks by refining the process so that students have key questions to answer. For example, instead of asking students to 'research the life of a famous artist', provide students with key questions to direct the task.

Depending on the ability of students, it might be appropriate to provide research sources or appropriate information. Students can be given specific assistance in locating one or more of these sources.

Written advice

Avoid giving homework orally. It should be placed on the board or overhead. Allow adequate time for students to copy it down. Check that it is accurately recorded in the students' record books.

Preteaching

Preteaching is the most powerful strategy for assisting comprehension and making maximum use of class time. For more on this, see 'Preteaching', Chapter 6.

Linking concepts

Link new concepts with previous knowledge. Make implicit (hidden) information quite explicit. LLD students find it difficult to interpret information that is not absolutely explicit.

Evaluation by criterion sheets

Criterion sheets are an excellent tool to help students stay on task and to complete all parts of the task successfully. Criterion sheets:

- make each step of the task clear;
- give a checklist of stages for the task;
- provide a structure to allow students to think about each step and whether they have completed it;
- provide an opportunity for students to reflect on their learning and whether they were able to complete each section properly.

Figure 14.1 is an example of an evaluation sheet that reflects an evaluation of the process that students have completed.

Figure 14.1 Evaluation sheet

Evaluation Sheet

I have listed keywords and used these keywords to form headings and subheadings for my research.

Always	Mostly	Sometimes	Not anywhere

Note-taking

I have recorded my notes in point form using appropriate headings and subheadings.

Always	Mostly	Sometimes	Not anywhere

I have used colour coding to show different resources.

Always	Mostly	Sometimes	Not anywhere

I have used ticks [✓] when I have found information in more than one resource.

Always	Mostly	Sometimes	Not anywhere

Synthesis [putting it all together]

I have written my notes into sentences under headings.

Always	Mostly	Sometimes	Not anywhere

My work shows that I understand special words and phrases used in this topic. For special words, I have included a definition.

Always	Mostly	Sometimes	Not anywhere

My notes and final report includes some of my own conclusions.

Always	Mostly	Sometimes	Not anywhere

Presentation

My report is presented using headings and subheadings to help the reader follow my ideas. I have included a contents page.

Always	Mostly	Sometimes	Not anywhere

I have used a range of resources [not just Encarta Encyclopedia] and recorded these in the correct format.

Always	Mostly	Sometimes	Not anywhere

I have used accurate spelling and expression.

Always	Mostly	Sometimes	Not anywhere

Sue Healey, Tintern AGGS

CHAPTER **15**

How to Modify Tests, Assessments, and Reports

Tests

Tests are a daunting experience for students with LLD. If teachers modify tests, students are supported, their stress is reduced, they can perform to their best and they are learning the skills to approach the test situation.

Teachers can consider the following strategies:

- open-book tests in which students bring prepared notes or books into the test;
- substitution of oral tests for written tests;
- providing an opportunity for students to ask for test questions to be read;
- providing an opportunity for students to ask for a clarification of questions;
- providing a scribe to write down students' answers;
- substituting cloze sentence completion tasks for written answers;
- providing the possibility of underlining or circling alternatives, rather than writing them out;
- preparation of alternative tests that have some more difficult questions deleted;
- alteration of multiple-choice questions to give only two or three choices (multiple-choice questions can be difficult if there are no clues available from the context);
- putting all questions in the positive ('which one is correct?') rather than the negative ('which one is incorrect?');
- on appropriate occasions, allow students the option of not taking a given test (this being preferable to dismal failure);
- allowing the use of 'props' (such as calculators, tables cards, word-processors, and spell-checkers);
- marking the test out of questions answered, rather than out of the total number of questions asked;
- not penalising spelling or grammar errors;
- not giving tests verbally (without other non-verbal cues to assist in understanding); and

- not imposing time limits that pressure students to work quickly; rather, encouraging students to complete what they can within the given time.

With regard to the last of these, in junior levels it is best to impose no time limit, but this is not practical when students are sitting a common test.

Figure 15.1 shows an original science test paper, and Figure 15.2 illustrates a revised test paper that incorporates some of the ideas listed above.

Figure 15.1 Original science test paper

Test – Reactions around us

Name: _____   Total: _____/60

Part A: True/false (Circle the correct answer.)

1. Physical changes are difficult to reverse.   T   F

2. A glowing splint placed into carbon dioxide gas will glow
   more brightly or re-ignite.   T   F

3. Oxygen gas turns limewater milky.   T   F

4. A precipitate is an insoluble substance formed by mixing two liquids.   T   F

5. Elements are composed of two or more compounds.   T   F

6. Air is an example of a mixture.   T   F

7. A catalyst is a substance that speeds up a chemical reaction
   but is itself unaffected.   T   F

8. The symbols He, Li, Ag, Na, and H stand for helium, lithium, silver,
   nitrogen, and hydrogen in that order.   T   F

9. Elements are made of only one type of atom.   T   F

10. 'Malleable' is a property of metals. It means they are shiny.   T   F

11. A periodic table is a table showing all the compounds that exist.   T   F

12. A metal conducts electricity.   T   F

13. Carbon is a common element found in the body.   T   F

14. The 'pop' test is used to detect hydrogen gas.   T   F

15. The atomic number tells us the number of protons.   T   F

Science Department, Tintern AGGS

Figure 15.2 Revised science test paper

Test – Reactions around us

Name: _____

Part A: True/false (Circle the correct answer.)

1.	Physical changes are difficult to reverse (change back).	T	F
2.	If you put a glowing match into carbon dioxide gas, it will glow more brightly or flame up (re-ignite).	T	F
3.	Oxygen gas turns limewater milky.	T	F
4.	When you mix two liquids together they form a precipitate that does not dissolve (is insoluble).	T	F
5.	Elements are made up of two or more compounds.	T	F
6.	Air is an example of a mixture.	T	F
7.	A catalyst is something that can speed up a chemical reaction but the catalyst does not change in any way.	T	F
8.	The symbol He stands for helium	T	F
	Li stands for lithium	T	F
	Ag stands for silver	T	F
	H stands for hydrogen	T	F
9.	There is only one type of atom in an element.	T	F
10.	If a metal is malleable it means that it is shiny.	T	F
11.	A periodic table shows all the elements that exist.	T	F
12.	Metals can conduct electricity.	T	F
13.	Carbon is a common element found in the body.	T	F
14.	The 'pop' test is used to detect hydrogen gas.	T	F
15.	The atomic number of an element tells us the number of protons that an element has.	T	F

15 marks

Florence Gough

Figure 15.3 shows an original diseases unit test paper, and Figure 15.4 illustrates a revised test paper that incorporates some of the ideas listed above.

Figure 15.3 Year 8 Diseases unit test

Diseases unit test

Read each question carefully before you try to answer.
Complete the questions you can do first.
Return to the more difficult questions.
Check your answers when you have finished.
Now begin.

Q1. List the five factors that can cause disease. Give an example of a disease that could be caused by each of the factors. Place your answers in the table below.

Factor	Example of disease
1.	
2.	
3.	
4.	
5.	

Q2. Explain how you could tell if someone was unwell. Write down three signs or symptoms.

1. _____

2. _____

3. _____

Diane Grochowska

Figure 15.4 Year 8 Diseases unit modified test

Diseases unit test

Read each question carefully before you try to answer.
Complete the questions you can do first.
Return to the more difficult questions.
Check your answers when you have finished.
Now begin.

Q1. List the five factors that can cause disease by completing the sentences below. Use the words in the box to help you.

diet   stress   genetic   life-style   bacteria   environment   age   infections

1. _____ – caused by bacteria and viruses.

2. _____ – as people get older some parts do not work as well.

3. _____ – poisons in our air and water.

4. _____ – poor diet, stress, and drugs.

5. _____ – some babies are born with an illness.

Q2. Explain how you could tell if someone was unwell. Write down three signs or symptoms.

1. _____

2. _____

3. _____

Diane Grochowska

Assessments

Some of the matters noted above can also be useful when assessing assignments.

When reporting on the progress of LLD students it is important that everyone is clear about the levels of assistance that students are receiving. It is vital that both the parents and the students are consulted *before* assistance is given. This is necessary to ensure that students and parents have realistic expectations of what can be achieved. Such consultation can also assist students to develop personal insight into their needs.

It might be appropriate for students to receive an assessment of 'satisfactory' or 'not satisfactory' – rather than a formal grade. One school uses an asterisk above a grade in a report to indicate that the assessment is modified.

Figures 15.5 and 15.6 show examples of reports.

Figure 15.5 Assessment key for reports

Assessment key for reports

Graded tasks

A	= Work is of an excellent standard
B	= Work is of a good standard
C	= Work is of a satisfactory standard
D	= Work is of a minimum acceptable standard
E	= Work is below the acceptable standard
F	= Work is significantly below the acceptable standard

S/N	= SATISFACTORY / NON-SATISFACTORY COMPLETION OF WORK TASKS
NS	= WORK NOT SUBMITTED

The following symbols are also used

+	= Higher standard within level of achievement
*	= Grade achieved with assistance
LS	= Late submission not graded
ABS	= Absent during task
NA	= Not assessed

Tintern AGGS

Figure 15.6 Geography report

Geography

Name _____   Form _____

This course involves the study of physical and urban geography, using both British and Asian case studies as the basis of comparing different aspects of the areas. Geography in third year focuses on the location of Britain and Asia in the world; water as a resource and weather and climate. The history and development of a British city and an Asian city provide a human dimension to the course. Students consolidate their geography skills through map work, graph work, statistical and data analysis and interpretation.

Areas of assessment	Level of achievement
Class work/Homework	S*
Research tasks	B+*
Class tests	C*

Approach to studies	
Level of application	1
Organisation	1
Participation in class	1

Comments

I am extremely pleased with the effort _____ has put into this subject over the semester. She is a delightful student who has approached her work with interest and enthusiasm. With support, her written work and assignments were of a very good standard in both content and presentation. She worked very hard to ensure all the set criteria were met. Test results reflect _____ has difficulty with interpreting and analysing data and information. Despite this, she always puts in an enormous effort. She consistently seeks assistance when having difficulty with the work and I wish her well for next year. She is friendly and polite at all times.

Tintern AGGS

References and Further Reading

Chapter 1 Language Development and LLD – What Goes Wrong?

Levine M. D. and Swartz C.W. (1997) 'The Unsuccessful Adolescent', <www.ldanatl.org/articles/seab/levine1.shtml>.

Lord Larson, V. (1995) *Language Disorders in Older Students: Preadolescents and Adolescents*, Eau Claire, WI: Thinking Publications.

Chapter 3 Adolescence and LLD – A Potent Mix

Pipher, Mary (1996) *Reviving Ophelia: Saving the Selves of Adolescent Girls*, Melbourne: Doubleday.

Prior, Margot, Sanson, Ann, Smart, Diana and Oberklaid, Frank (1983–2000) *Pathways from Infancy to Adolescence: Australian Temperament Project 1983–2000*, Melbourne: Australian Institute of Family Studies.

Chapter 4 Social Skills and Language

Bernstein, Deena. K. and Tiegerman-Farber, Ellenmorris (1997) *Language and Communication Disorders in Children*, Needham Heights, MA: Allyn and Bacon.

Freeman, Sabrina and Dake, Lorelei (1997) *Teach Me Language. A Language Manual*, Langley, BC: SKF Books.

Gerber, Adele (1993) *Language Related Learning Disabilities: their nature and treatment*, Baltimore, MD: Paul H. Brookes Publishing Company.

Levine, Mel (1996) *Educational Care*, Cambridge MA: Educators Publishing Services Inc.

Wiig, Elisabeth (1989) *Steps to Language Competence*, New York: Harcourt Brace Jovanovich.

Chapter 6 Preteaching

Lee, Harper (1989) *To Kill a Mockingbird*, London: Mandarin Paperbacks.

Swanson, H. L. (1993) 'Learning disabilities from the perspective of cognitive psychology', in G. R. Lyon, D. B. Gray, J. P. Kavanagh and H. Krasnegor (eds), *Better Understanding Learning Disabilities: New Views from Research and their Implications for Education and Public Policies*, Baltimore, MD: Paul H. Brookes Publishing Co., pp. 199–228.

Swanson, Cooney and Overholser (1989) cited in Swanson 1993 (op. cit.).

Wong and Jones (1982) cited in Swanson 1993 (op. cit.).

Chapter 7 Reading

Bitton Jackson, Livia (1994) *Elli Coming of Age in the Holocaust,* London: HarperCollins.

Hodgson Burnett, Frances (1961) *A Little Princess* (first published 1905), London: Penguin Books.

Ireland, Julie (1995) *A Kind of Dreaming*, Pymble, NSW: HarperCollins.

Lee, Harper (1989) *To Kill a Mockingbird,* London: Mandarin Paperbacks, p. 66.

Marsden, John (1990) *So Much to Tell You* (first published 1987), Glebe, NSW: Walter McVitty Books.

Parsons, Malcolm (1996) *Heinemann Outcomes Science 2*, Melbourne: Rigby Heinemann, p. 70.

Tallal, P. (1988) 'Developmental Language Disorders: Part 1: Definition', *Human Communication Canada*, 12, 7–22.

Twain, Mark (1995) *The Adventures of Tom Sawyer*, New York: Viking, p. 37.

Chapter 8 Libraries and Research

Wong, Bernice (1997) 'Research on genre-specific strategies for enhancing writing in adolescents with learning disabilities', *Learning Disability Quarterly*, Volume 20, Spring 1997, pp. 140–59.

Chapter 9 Skills across the Curriculum

Brent, M., Gough, F. and Robinson, S. (1988) 'Adolescent language-learning disabilities theoretical and practical issues', unpublished bound notes for use by professional colleagues; further information available from present authors.

Eshuys, J., Guest, V. and Lawrence, J. (1991) *Discovering the Ancient World*, Milton, Qld: Jacaranda Wiley Ltd.

Chapter 10 Writing

Bell, Nanci (1991) *Visualizing and Verbalizing: for Language Comprehension and Thinking*, Paso Robles, CA: Academy of Reading Publications.

Collins Cobuild English Dictionary (1997) London: HarperCollins.

Crystal, D. (1979) 'Working with LARSP', New York: Elsevier, cited in Westby, C. E. (1989) 'Assessing and remediating text comprehension problems' in Kanhai, A.G. and Catts, H. W. (eds), *Reading Disabilities: A Developmental Language Perspective*. Boston: College Hill, pp. 199–259.

Englert, C. S. (1992) 'Writing instruction from a sociocultural perspective: the holistic, dialogic and social enterprise of writing', in Wong, B. Y. L. (ed.), 'Cognitive process-based instruction', *Journal of Learning Disabilities*, 25(3), 153–72.

Herald Sun, Melbourne (1998) 'Whales Trucked to Safer Waters', 19 October.

Hughes, Ted (1989) *Selected Poems 1957–1981*, London: Faber and Faber, p. 15.

Lane, Sarah and Darby, Max (1998) *Art is ...* Milton, Qld: Jacaranda Wiley Ltd .

Lee, Harper (1989) *To Kill a Mockingbird*, London: Mandarin Paperbacks.

Magorian, Michelle (1996) *Goodnight Mr Tom*, Harmondsworth: Penguin.

Schumaker, J. B., Nolan, S. M. and Deshler, D. D. (1985) *The Error Monitoring Strategy: Learning Strategies Curriculum*, Lawrence, University of Kansas, cited in Wong (1997), op. cit.

Scott, C. M. (1989) 'Problem Writers: Nature, Assessment, and Intervention', in Kamhai, A.G. and Catts, H. W. (eds), *Reading Disabilities: A Developmental Language Perspective*, Boston: College Hill, pp. 303–44.

Thiele, Colin (1966) *Storm Boy*, Dee Why West, NSW. Rigby Publishers, p. 72.

Twain, Mark (1995) *The Adventures of Tom Sawyer*, New York: Viking

Westby, C.E. (1989) 'Assessing and remediating text comprehension problems', in Kamhai, A.G. and Catts, H. W. (eds), *Reading Disabilities: A Developmental Language Perspective*, Boston: College Hill, pp. 199–259.

Wong, Bernice (1997) 'Research on genre-specific strategies for enhancing writing in adolescents with learning disabilities', *Learning Disability Quarterly*, Volume 20, Spring 1997, pp. 140–59.

Chapter 12 Framework for Modifying Curriculum

Lavoie, Richard (1989) 'How difficult can this be?', The FAT City Video, Peter Rosen Productions, Greenwich, USA.

Levine, M. D. and Swartz, C.W. (1997) 'The Unsuccessful Adolescent', <www.ldanatl.org/articles/seab/levine1.shtml

Loertscher, David (1996) 'All that glitters may not be gold', *Emergency Librarian* (now *Teacher Librarian: The Journal for School Library Professionals*), vol. 24, no. 2.

School Library Association of Victoria (1995) with assistance from the Australian Library and Information Association Schools Section (Victorian Group), *Using the CSF to Teach Information Skills*, published by author, Richmond, Victoria, Australia.

Chapter 13 How to Modify the Amount of Work

Brent, M., Gough, F. and Robinson, S. (1988) 'Adolescent language-learning disabilities theoretical and practical issues', unpublished bound notes for use by professional colleagues; further information available from present authors.

Parsons, Malcolm (1996) *Heinemann Outcomes Science 2*, Melbourne: Rigby Heinemann, p. 81.

Appendix

The Jaguar

The apes yawn and adore their fleas in the sun,
The parrots shriek as if they were on fire, or strut
Like cheap tarts to attract the stroller with the nut.
Fatigued with indolence, tiger and lion

Lie still as the sun. The boa-constrictor's coil
Is a fossil. Cage after cage seems empty, or
Stinks of sleepers from the breathing straw.
It might be painted on a nursery wall.

But who runs like the rest past these arrives
At a cage where the crowd stands, stares, mesmerised,
As a child at a dream, at a jaguar hurrying, enraged
Through prison darkness after the drills of his eyes

On a short fierce fuse. Not in boredom –
The eye satisfied to be blind in fire,
By the bang of the blood in the brain deaf the ear –
He spins from the bars, but there's no cage to him

More than to the visionary in his cell:
His stride is wildernesses of freedom:
The world rolls under the long thrust of his hell.
Over the cage floor the horizons come.

Hughes, T. (1982). 'The Jaguar' in *Selected Poems 1957–1981*, London, Faber and Faber Ltd, p. 15.

Index

writing xii *see also* written language

Writing difficulties, checklist for *79–80*

written language

    brainstorming to assist 72–3, *74–5*, 75

    characteristics of 65

    checklist for difficulties with *79–80*

    checksheets aiding *78*, 78–9, *79–80*

    comprehension influencing 69–70, 71–2

    during adolescence 2, 65–7

    keywords and ideas assisting 76, *77–8*, 78

    limitations of LLD students 90–2

    poor handwriting affecting 91–2

    purpose of 67–8

    skill development goals 92

    teaching strategies 75–6, 92

    use of computers for 91, 92

    vocabulary affecting 70–2

    see also essays

written tests *see* tests

Yellow Pages 95